W9-AOM-852

JOHN C. GOLD

TWENTY-FIRST CENTURY BOOKS
A Division of Henry Holt and Company
New York

I dedicate this book to my dad, the beaver dam and the woods.

Twenty-First Century Books
A Division of Henry Holt and Company, Inc.
115 West 18th Street
New York, NY 10011

Henry Holt® and colophon are trademarks of
Henry Holt and Company, Inc.
Publishers since 1866

Published in Canada by Fitzhenry & Whiteside Ltd.
195 Allstate Parkway, Markham, Ontario, L3R 4T8

Library of Congress Cataloging-in-Publication Data
Gold, John C.
Environments of the Western Hemisphere / John C. Gold. — 1st ed.
p. cm. — (Comparing continents)
Includes bibliographical references and index.
Summary: Describes the land and physical environment of the Western Hemisphere, discusses ways in which people adapt to and shape their environments, and suggests responsible policies for the future.
1. Western Hemisphere—Environmental conditions—Juvenile literature. 2. Environmental management—Western Hemisphere—Juvenile literature.
I. Title. II. Series.
GE160.W47G65 1997
363.7'009181'2—dc21 97–15659
CIP
AC

Photo Credits
Cover photographs and photographs on pages 3, 8 (Jeremy Woodhouse), 15, 16, 20, 25, 27, 30, 34, 36, 40, 43, 48, 51, 52, 55, 58, 60, 61, 62, 64, 72, 77 (Russ Illig), 80, 82, and 84 © PhotoDisc.
Photographs on pages 19, 41, 66, and 85 © 1997 John C. Gold.
Photographs on page 45 © Francis Walton.
Photograph on page 68 © Byron Augustin/Tom Stack & Associates.
Maps on pages 4, 12, 18, 23, and 29 © 1997 Susan D. Gold.

Design, Typesetting, and Layout
Custom Communications

ISBN 0-8050-5601-7
First Edition 1997

Printed in Mexico.
All first editions are printed on acid-free paper ∞.
1 3 5 7 9 10 8 6 4 2

CONTENTS

INTRODUCTION *Many Environments* 5

CHAPTER ONE *The Physical Environment* 9

CHAPTER TWO *Adapting to the Environment* 35

CHAPTER THREE *Shaping the Environment* 49

CHAPTER FOUR *Paying the Bill* 63

CHAPTER FIVE *Solutions for the Future* 83

GLOSSARY 89

SOURCE NOTES 91

FURTHER READING 94

INDEX 95

MAPS

Western Hemisphere 4

Canada 12

United States 18

Mexico/Central America 23

South America 29

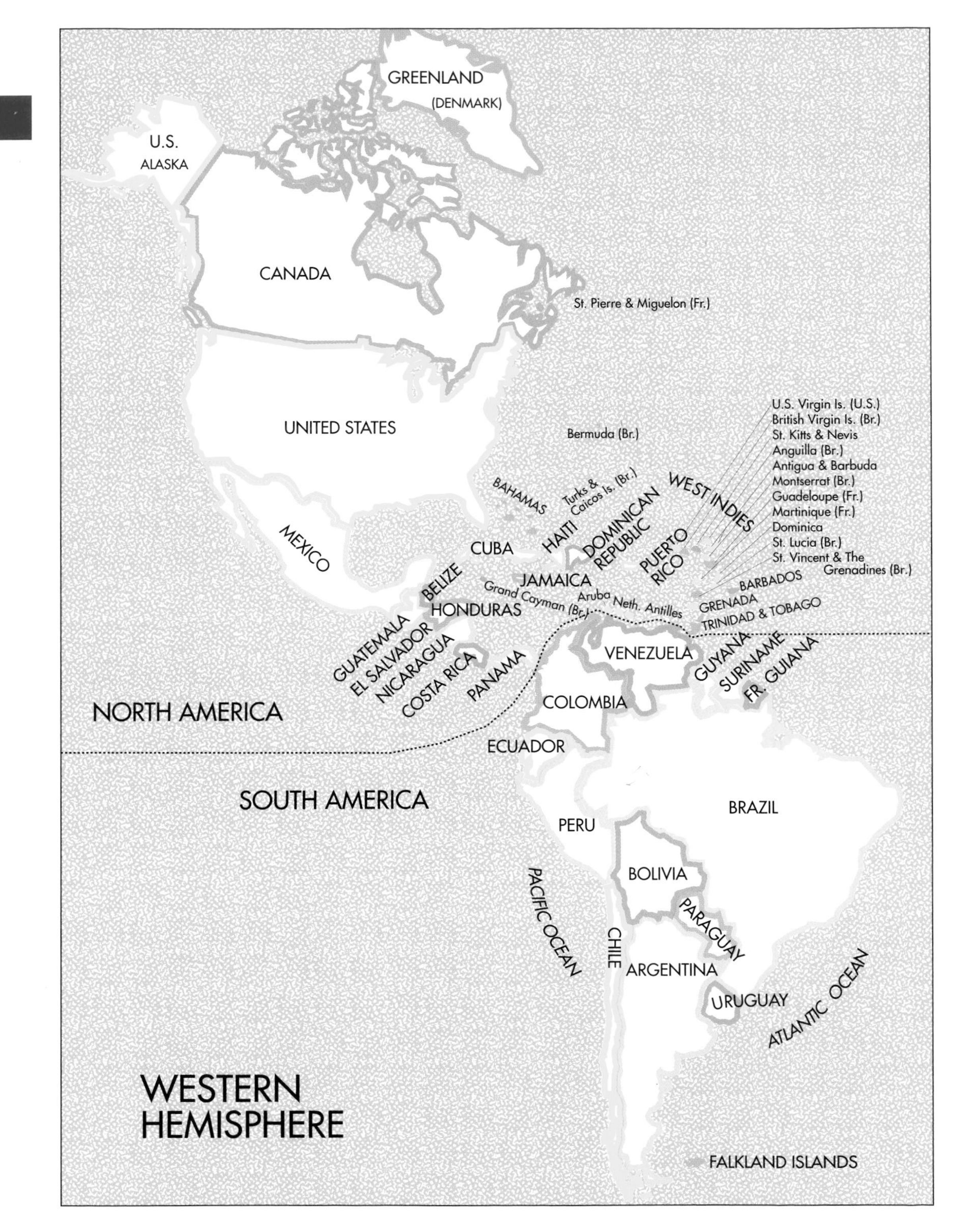
GREENLAND
(DENMARK)
U.S.
ALASKA
CANADA
St. Pierre & Miguelon (Fr.)
UNITED STATES
Bermuda (Br.)
U.S. Virgin Is. (U.S.)
British Virgin Is. (Br.)
St. Kitts & Nevis
Anguilla (Br.)
Antigua & Barbuda
Montserrat (Br.)
Guadeloupe (Fr.)
Martinique (Fr.)
Dominica
St. Lucia (Br.)
St. Vincent & The Grenadines (Br.)
BAHAMAS
Turks & Caicos Is. (Br.)
WEST INDIES
MEXICO
CUBA
HAITI
DOMINICAN REPUBLIC
PUERTO RICO
BELIZE
JAMAICA
Grand Cayman (Br.)
Aruba
Neth. Antilles
BARBADOS
GRENADA
TRINIDAD & TOBAGO
HONDURAS
GUATEMALA
EL SALVADOR
NICARAGUA
COSTA RICA
PANAMA
VENEZUELA
GUYANA
SURINAME
FR. GUIANA
NORTH AMERICA
COLOMBIA
ECUADOR
SOUTH AMERICA
BRAZIL
PERU
BOLIVIA
PACIFIC OCEAN
PARAGUAY
CHILE
ARGENTINA
URUGUAY
ATLANTIC OCEAN
WESTERN HEMISPHERE
FALKLAND ISLANDS

INTRODUCTION

MANY ENVIRONMENTS

The environments of the Western Hemisphere span a wide range of lands, temperatures, and climates. In the north is the permanently frozen tundra of the Canadian territories. Farther south are the hot, damp jungles of the South American rain forest. On the eastern edge of the United States, the coastal plain lies only a few feet above sea level in some areas. Yet along the western coast of South America, the towering Andes Mountains rise so high the air is too thin for most people to live there.

Despite this variation, humans have managed to find homes for themselves almost everywhere in the Western Hemisphere. Whether shivering in the coldest Arctic village or sweating in palm-roofed huts in the soggy Amazon, people have managed to adapt to the different environments.

Over the years, the style of adaptation has changed. The first inhabitants of the Western Hemisphere, who lived here before the Europeans arrived, adapted their lives to the conditions imposed by the environment. Many were hunters and gatherers, living off the animals and plants found in their region. Others developed styles of agriculture that existed in harmony with the land.

The European settlers, who began arriving in the Western Hemisphere in the fifteenth century, brought a different way of interacting with the environment. Over the centuries that followed, these settlers and their descendants shaped the environment to fit their needs. They cut down forests to make room for fields and dammed rivers for irrigation, flood control, and energy. Their numbers, and thus their needs for housing and food, were greater than those of the original inhabitants, the Native Americans.

The ability to reshape the environment allowed the new settlers to flourish. Their population grew far beyond that of the Native Americans. But in many cases this reshaping has strained the environment beyond its capacity. We are discovering that our ability to rearrange the environment has had unexpected—and, in some cases, devastating—side effects.

Today, near the end of the twentieth century, we have wasted or destroyed much of the bounty given to us by nature. Oceans, lakes, and rivers are being emptied of fish and polluted by toxic waste. Forests are cut down and burned. Wetlands are filled with dirt for shopping centers and crop lands. Our constant need for energy is producing air pollution that chokes us and creates acid rain that destroys lakes and trees and damages man-made structures. Some people believe this air pollution may also be causing the temperature of the planet to rise.

Now, after many years of misusing our environment, we are beginning to realize we must treat it more carefully. Dirty air and disappearing species have made us understand that the earth is not the unlimited resource we once thought. As we notice the loss of our forests and the warming of our planet, we have begun to take some steps to live in harmony with nature and to protect the environment that sustains us.

Some people say it may already be too late. They say the human race has set in motion a chain of events that cannot be stopped. Someday, they say, our planet will become so warm that areas that are now frozen will melt, causing oceans to rise and flood parts of the world. Climate changes brought on by human activity will cause once fertile lands to dry up and become deserts.

Others say it is too early to predict that these dire events will occur. These people say we can alter our habits to prevent further damage to the air, water, and land around us. Everyone agrees, however, that human activities are affecting the environment and that the problems caused by these actions must be faced.

CHAPTER ONE

THE PHYSICAL ENVIRONMENT

The Western Hemisphere is made up of two continents (North America and South America) and five major political regions: Canada, the United States, Mexico, Central America, and South America. Mexico, Central America, and South America are often thought of as one region called Latin America, because they share a similar culture. The land of the Western Hemisphere stretches unbroken from the North Pole almost to the continent of Antarctica, which sits over the South Pole.

The environments of the hemisphere vary greatly depending upon the region. Generally, however, climates are colder and harsher in the northern part of the hemisphere. Regions farther south have a more temperate, milder, climate. Near the equator, the climate becomes warm and tropical. In the far south it once again turns cold in some areas.

The Western Hemisphere has a varied terrain, from mountains (pictured at left) to deserts to frozen tundra to lush tropical isles.

Canada is the northernmost nation in the Western

WESTERN HEMISPHERE ENVIRONMENTAL FACTS

Highest mountain in South America: Mt. Aconcagua on Chile-Argentina border, 23,034 feet

Highest mountain in North America: Mt. McKinley in Alaska, 20,320 feet

Lowest point in South America: Valdes Peninsula, Argentina, 131 feet below sea level

Lowest point in North America: Death Valley, California, US, 282 feet below sea level

Largest man-made lake formed by a dam in South America: Guri (Raul Leoni) Dam in Venezuela, 136,000 cubic meters

Largest man-made lake formed by a dam in North America: Daniel Johnson Dam in Canada, 141,852 cubic meters

Largest freshwater lake in the world: Lake Superior on Canada-U.S. border, 31,820 sq. mi., 1,333 feet deep

Largest lake in South America: Titicaca Lake on Bolivia-Peru border, 3,141 sq. mi., 1,214 feet deep

Hemisphere. It also has the most land of any country in the hemisphere, stretching from the Arctic Ocean in the north to the United States in the south. On the east it reaches to the Atlantic Ocean, and on the west it touches the Pacific Ocean. Greenland also lies in the northern part of the hemisphere, with two-thirds of the island north of the Arctic Circle. Its climate and environment are similar to the Canadian north.

The United States begins on the southern border of Canada and continues south to the Gulf of Mexico and the border of Mexico. It, too, spans from the Atlantic to the Pacific Ocean.

Mexico stretches from the southern United States border to the countries of Guatemala and Belize in the south. On the east coast it is bordered by the Gulf of Mexico and the Caribbean Sea, and on the west coast it is bordered by the Pacific Ocean. Canada, the United States, and Mexico are all part of the continent of North America.

Central America is an isthmus, a narrow strip of land that links Mexico with the South American continent. Central America consists of seven countries. On the east lies the Caribbean Sea; the Pacific Ocean is on the west.

In the Caribbean Sea a chain of islands stretches from the southern tip of Florida to the northeastern coast of South America near Venezuela. Called the West Indies, this chain includes the Bahamas, Jamaica, Puerto Rico, and a number of other islands. These islands and others in the region, as well as Central

America are technically considered to be part of North America. They share a tropical climate.

South America stretches from the southern border of Central America almost to the continent of Antarctica. It is bordered on the north by the Caribbean Sea, on the east by the Atlantic Ocean, and on the west by the Pacific Ocean.

The environment of an area is controlled by many factors. The geography, or physical layout of the land, plays a large part in determining the type of environment found in a certain area. The countries of the Western Hemisphere each have a wide variety of geography. This variety gives each country several different kinds of environments.

Canada's Lands

In land area, Canada is the largest country in the Western Hemisphere. It is also the second largest country in the world, smaller only than Russia. Canada covers more than three-and-one-half million square miles and has wide variations in climate and habitats. Some parts of the country are so cold for so much of the year that the ground never completely thaws. Other parts are warm enough to grow grains and even some fruit trees.

Canada is divided into six areas, based on the physical layout of the land. The largest area, in the center of the country, is called the Canadian Shield. It is a large, flat area similar to a plain and is surrounded by

Western Hemisphere Environmental Facts

Largest river in South America and second largest in world: Amazon River, 3,912 miles long

Largest river in North America: Mississippi-Missouri-Red Rock River in U.S., 3,880 miles long

Largest island in Western Hemisphere and largest in world: Greenland, 839,999 sq. mi.

Largest desert in Western Hemisphere and largest in world: Atacama Desert in Chile, 400 miles long

Highest recorded temperature in Western Hemisphere: 120°F in Rivadavia, Argentina, December 11, 1905

Lowest recorded temperature in North America: -87°F in Northice, Greenland, January 9, 1954

Lowest recorded temperature in South America: -27°F in Sarmiento, Argentina, January 1, 1907

Source: 1995 Information Please Almanac

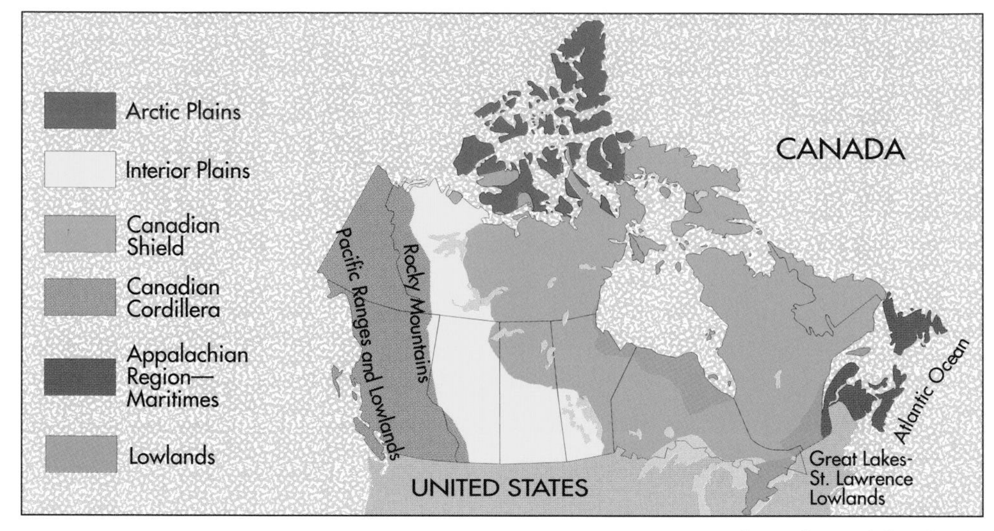

Source: *Compton's Encyclopedia*

mountains on the east and west. It covers one-half of the country. Parts of Ontario, Quebec, Manitoba, and the Northwest Territories are in the shield.

The shield was formed by massive glaciers covering that section of Canada about two million years ago. When the glaciers retreated, they scrubbed the land, leaving behind a landscape pockmarked with areas of shallow water and little soil that could be used to grow crops. The shield is one of Canada's least populated areas. Parts of it are so desolate they have been nicknamed the Barrens.[1]

To the west and south of the shield are the interior plains. These extend to the Rocky Mountains and are an extension of the Great Plains found in the United States. This area is known for its grassy prairies. The provinces of Alberta, Saskatchewan, and Manitoba, as well as part of British Columbia, lie in this area.

East of the shield is a flat, hilly area known as the Great Lakes-St. Lawrence Lowlands. Parts of the provinces of Quebec and Ontario are in this region.

East of the Great Lakes area and extending to the Atlantic Ocean is the Appalachian Region of Canada. This area is marked by a series of worn-down mountain ranges—the same range that extends into the United States. The provinces of Nova Scotia, Prince Edward Island, New Brunswick, and the island of Newfoundland are all in this area. This part of Canada is also called the Maritimes, because it is next to the ocean.

In the far west is a belt of mountains called the Canadian Cordillera. Cordillera is a term for a series of mountains. This mountain range extends five hundred miles from the Rocky Mountains to the Pacific Ocean. The cordillera is mostly unpopulated.

North of the shield are the Arctic plains and plateaus. These are areas where snow and ice exist all year long.

Climate in Canada

Canada's climates are somewhat linked to the different physical regions of the country, but not completely. The southern part of Canada has several types of temperate climates. A temperate climate is one with alternating seasons, like summer and winter. Along the Canadian Pacific coast, summers are cool with temperatures in the 60s, and winters are mild with temperatures in the 30s. The ocean helps to keep temperatures from getting too hot or too cold. This is also true along the Canadian east coast.

British Columbia, along the west coast, has a lot of rainfall, up to 160 inches in some areas. Rainfall in the Atlantic provinces averages forty inches, from a low of seventeen inches per year in parts of Newfoundland to a high of 114 inches in New Brunswick.

Inland, in the southern interior plains, the summers are slightly warmer and the winters cooler, with temperatures dropping to below zero at times. Rainfall averages between fifteen and twenty inches a year.

The Great Lakes-St. Lawrence Lowlands and the Appalachian Region have a climate similar to that of the interior plains. These regions, however, have slightly more rain than the plains, a yearly average of twenty-eight inches.

The northern part of Canada has an Arctic climate, which is marked by very long, cold winters and short, cool summers. The average temperature in the winter is far below zero. In the summer the highest temperature never gets above 50°F. Temperatures as low as -81° F have been recorded in parts of the Yukon Territory. In these areas the ground never thaws more than a few inches down from the surface. This frozen section of land is called permafrost. In some places the ground is frozen to more than one thousand feet deep. Despite their image as snow-covered lands, Canada's Northwest Territories and Yukon regions have light precipitation, with as little as ten inches of rain a year (though one inch of rain generally equals about ten inches of snow).

Between the Arctic north and settled south are areas that have subarctic climates. These regions also have long, cold winters, but summers are warmer there than in the more northern Yukon Territory.

Canadian Vegetation and Natural Resources

Forests make up the majority of vegetation in Canada, covering 65 percent of the country. The northern forest is one of the largest in the world, and its trees are cut for lumber and paper. Canada is the world's largest source of newsprint, the thin paper used for newspapers. The trees in Canada's north are mostly evergreens, such as spruce and balsam. Farther south, around the Great Lakes and St. Lawrence Seaway, the forests are made up of hardwoods.

Above, logs cut from Quebec forests await transport to market.

The second largest category of vegetation is tundra. This covers 20 percent of the country, all in the northern section. Tundra is a mixture of low-growing plants that include shrubs that bear berries and fast-growing mosses and lichens (a type of fungus that grows on rocks or tree trunks). All these plants can survive in areas where the growing season is short and the soil poor. This type of vegetation is found in parts of the Canadian shield and in subarctic climates.

Grasslands make up the last large block of vegetation, about 10 percent. These are mostly found in the interior parts of the prairies where there is not enough

At right, the wheat fields of Manitoba

rain to support forests. In many of these areas, however, crops planted by humans have replaced the native prairie grasses.

Only 5 percent of the country's land is suitable for agriculture,[2] but that hasn't kept the Canadian people from making the most of what they have. Canada is one of the world's leading producers of grains. The prairie provinces of Alberta, Saskatchewan, and Manitoba grow wheat, barley, and oats. Tobacco and fruit grow in parts of southern Ontario.

Canada has many natural resources that are mined for the country's own use and for export. It is a leading producer of several minerals including nickel, zinc, asbestos, uranium, and molybdenum (a hard, gray metallic element used to strengthen certain kinds of metals). These minerals are important in the economy of countries around the world. Canada also has supplies of petroleum and natural gas that are produced in large enough quantities to export.

Canada is a seafaring nation, and for centuries the Canadian people along the coasts have made their living from the sea. On Canada's east coast and the island of Newfoundland, much of the fish is caught on the Grand Banks, a shallow section of the Atlantic Ocean where fish gather to feed and reproduce.

U.S. Lands

Lying between Canada and Mexico in the middle of the North American continent, the United States has a widely varied geography. Yet overall, the lay of the land in the United States is more hospitable to humans than that in Canada.

The United States has five main geographic areas. Along the east and south coasts of the country is the Atlantic Plain. This is a broad platform that starts at the Appalachian Mountains and extends eastward to the coast and then another two hundred miles out under the Atlantic Ocean. The section that extends underneath the sea is called the Continental Shelf. This was once one of the richest fishing grounds in the world.[3]

The plain runs from the New England region in the Northeast, south along the east coast, around the coast of Florida, and along the Gulf of Mexico in the south. Most of the plain is less than three hundred feet above sea level.

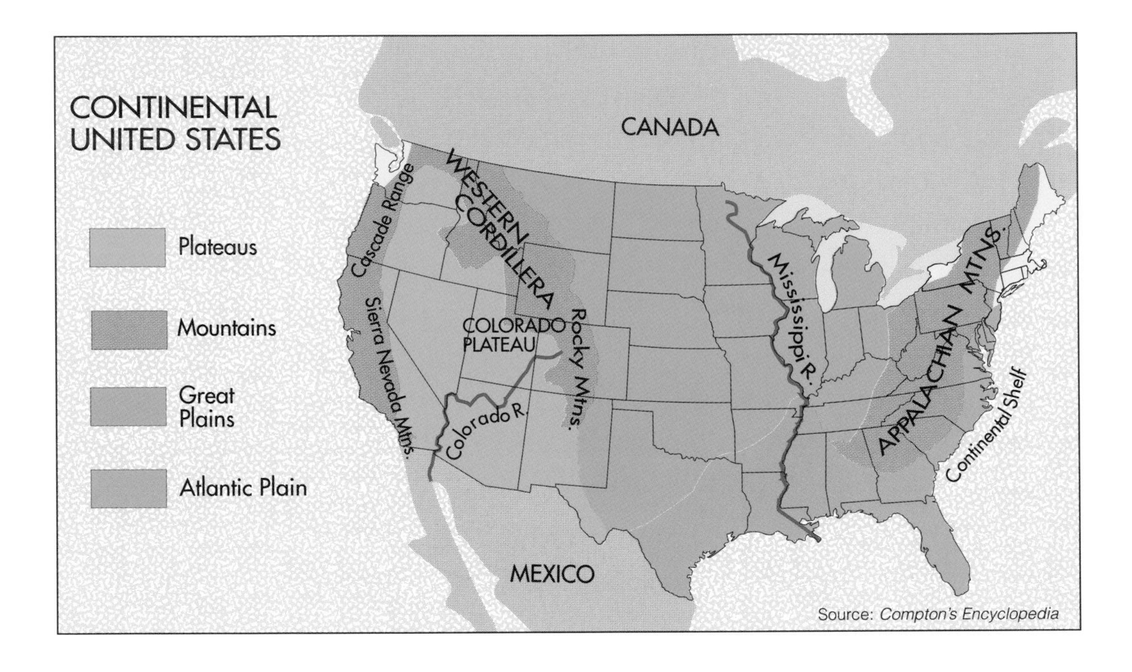

Source: *Compton's Encyclopedia*

West of the Atlantic Plain is the Appalachian mountain system. This is a belt of mountains that runs from the state of Alabama into Canada. Parts of this region are rich in coal and have been heavily mined.

Farther west are the Great Plains, a lowland plain that runs from the Appalachians to the Rocky Mountains. Wind-blown silt—fine soil created from the grinding action of ancient glaciers passing over the northern part of the country—has made the plains one of the best agricultural areas in the world.

West of the Great Plains is the Western Cordillera. This section of mountains and valleys runs the length of the country from north to south. There are several mountain ranges in the area. Those farthest east are the Rocky Mountains, which extend from the southwestern United States all the way into Canada. Farther west are a series of elevated plateaus. One of the more famous of these is the Colorado Plateau, which is cut by the Colorado River to form the Grand Canyon.

Farthest west, rising from the shores of the Pacific Ocean, are two more mountain ranges. The Sierra Nevada is in southern California. North of this, in the states of Oregon and Washington, is the Cascade Range. The mountains in this region include Mt. St. Helens, a volcano that erupted in 1980. Although Hawaii, a chain of islands 2,397 miles off the west coast, is part of the United States, it is not considered part of the Western Hemisphere.

Above, the Grand Canyon in Arizona displays a rainbow of multicolored rock exposed by the cutting action of the Colorado River.

U.S. Climate

The United States does not have the extremes in climate found in Canada, although the climate does vary with latitude and distance from the ocean. The northern parts of the country have longer and colder winters than those farther south. Areas closer to oceans have warmer winters and cooler summers than areas farther inland.

The northeastern part of the country has an average annual temperature of 55°F. In southern Florida, the average temperature is 75°F.

The Midwest has similar differences in temperature from north to south. Minneapolis, Minnesota, in the northern part of the region, has an annual average temperature of 45°F. Tulsa, Oklahoma, which is 640 miles south of Minneapolis, has an annual average temperature of 61°F.

The differences between north and south are not as great on the west coast, where the ocean keeps temperatures mild. In the northwest, the average annual temperature is 54°F. The city of Los Angeles, in the south, has an average annual temperature of 63°F.

Below, a cloud of lava and steam spew from Mt. St. Helens in Washington.

Some parts of the country have unique weather conditions. Southern Florida, for example, has the only tropical climate in the continental United States. Here it is warm and humid all year long, although winters are somewhat cooler and drier than the rest of the year. Along the coast, sixty inches of rain falls annually. Inland, the climate is somewhat drier.

New England receives from thirty to forty-five inches of rain a year, while the mid-Atlantic region gets forty to fifty-five inches.

Parts of the southwest are very dry, or semi-arid. Limited rainfall creates a desert climate in several areas. Less than ten inches of rain falls in the Rocky Mountains. Along the western basins and plateaus, rainfall is scanty (only about ten inches a year) and usually falls in late summer and midwinter in the southern sections.

In the north central plains rainfall ranges from twenty to forty inches a year. Along the eastern edge of the Great Plains, annual rainfall measures about twenty inches. The western edge is drier, only ten inches a year with frequent droughts. The opposite is found in the northwest part of the country, where mild temperatures and heavy rainfall—up to one hundred inches a year—create conditions that support a type of rain forest. Farther down the Pacific coast, however, southern California receives only about ten inches of rain a year.

U.S. Vegetation and Natural Resources

The vegetation of the United States is as varied as its climates. In tropical and subtropical Florida, mangrove and palmetto trees grow, as well as fruit trees that bear oranges and grapefruit. The southeast region also produces tobacco and cotton.

Farther north along the coast are the pine forests of the Carolinas, Georgia peach trees, and the apple trees and mixed hardwood and evergreen forests of the Northeast.

To the west of the Appalachian Mountains are the grasslands of the Great Plains. Like the grasslands of Canada, much of the original vegetation has been plowed under for crop growth.

With its mostly hospitable climate, good soil, and beneficial geography, the United States has become an agricultural leader in the Western Hemisphere. Farmers have taken advantage of the rich soil of the Midwest to raise thousands of tons of corn, wheat, and soybeans, which are consumed in the United States and exported around the world. This part of the country is often referred to as "America's breadbasket" because of the wheat that is grown there.

Farther west are the evergreen forests of the Rocky

Mountains. In the northwestern portion of the country, enough rain falls to support a rain forest that has massive evergreen trees. In the arid southwestern section, vegetation is sparse, consisting mostly of shrubs and grasses. Parts of the dry western areas are used for agriculture, but they require extensive irrigation. Land too dry for agriculture is used for grazing cattle.

California, on the West Coast, is noted for its grapes, cotton, grains, strawberries, and vegetables. Tropical fruits and vegetables, sugar cane, pineapple, coffee, bananas, and nuts grow in Hawaii's fertile soil. All of this makes the United States a major exporter of food and agricultural products.

The forests of the Northwest, northern Midwest, and Northeast are logged for lumber and for pulpwood used to make paper. The state of Alaska, which is physically separated from the rest of the United States, is a source of petroleum from oil fields in the northern part of the state. Oil is also found in many of the western states, including Texas. The first commercial oil well in the world was drilled in Titusville, Pennsylvania, in 1859.

Like Canada, the United States harvests the oceans off its east and west coasts for fish. Both coasts of the country are home to many fishermen and businesses that process and sell the fish.

Mexico's Lands

Bordering on the southwest edge of the United

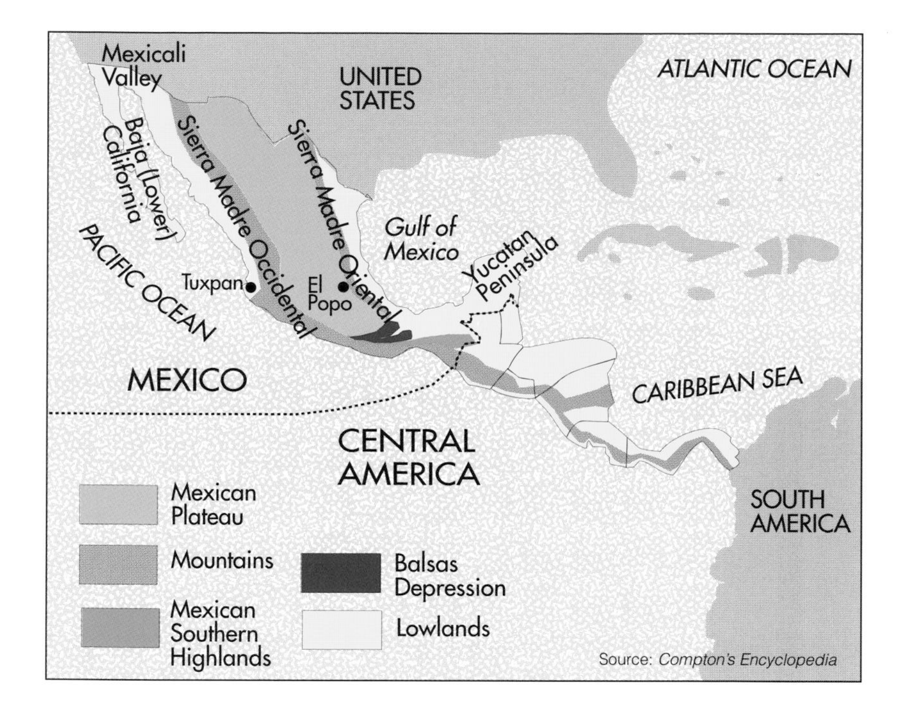

States is Mexico. Classified as part of North America, Mexico is also the northernmost country of Latin America.

Mountains are a major part of Mexico's landscape. Many of the mountains were formed by erupting volcanoes. Several of these volcanoes are still active.

Almost half of the country is dominated by the Mexican Plateau, a raised area that sits between two mountain ranges, the Sierra Madre Oriental on the east and the Sierra Madre Occidental on the west. This region has many lakes and a cooler climate than the lowlands. This section is also where most of the nation's crops grow.

To the east and west of the Mexican Plateau are the

'El Popo' Comes Alive

In May 1997, the Popocatepetl volcano in Mexico began showing signs of life. Several explosions emanated from the volcano, which also began spewing ash and steam into the air. One explosion sent red hot rocks flying into the air and set thirty-eight acres of land on fire. The blasts caused homes in the area to rattle.

Although the volcano's last major eruption happened more than twelve hundred years ago, the volcano has shown signs of life since then in 1920, 1994, and 1995. Each time, the volcano eventually quieted down without a full-scale eruption.

Residents who live near the 17,887-foot-high volcano told reporters they were used to its rumblings. But just to be safe, many climb the sides of the mountain and place offerings of fruit and other foods to appease the forces they believe control the volcano.

Scientists studying the volcano said they were not sure if it would erupt this time. They, like everyone else, have to wait, watch, and wonder what nature will finally do.

coastal lowlands. The Gulf Coastal Plain extends nine hundred miles along the Gulf of Mexico from Texas to the Yucatan Peninsula. The narrower Pacific coastal lowlands begin near Mexicali Valley in the north and end near Tuxpan, nine hundred miles to the south.

Mexico's Baja California peninsula is an extremely arid and isolated strip of land connected to the northern part of the country and extending south off the Pacific Coast. It is eight hundred miles long and never much wider than one hundred miles.

Two other minor sections are the Balsas Depression, a series of small, irregular basins south of the Mexican Plateau, and the Southern Highlands, a series of mountains in the southern part of the country.

Mexican Climate

Because of its geography, Mexico's climate and temperature vary mostly by altitude, with the hottest areas being along the coast.

In the southern coastal areas, Mexico has a tropical rain forest-type of climate. This hot, humid area receives more than eighty inches of rain a year and is called the *tierra caliente*, or "hot zone."

Higher up, on the Mexican Plateau, the climate is more temperate. Normal temperatures range from 54°F to 73°F. This climate is known by Mexicans as *tierra templada*, or "temperate zone."

Mexico's south receives more rainfall than the north, which is generally dry and has an arid climate.

Below, beach-goers enjoy the tropical weather in Cancún, Mexico, along the Gulf Coastal Plain of the Yucatan Peninsula.

Mexico's Vegetation and Natural Resources

Mexico's vegetation varies depending on its location in the country. In the southern coastal areas, warm, wet conditions support rain forest and tropical plants. At higher altitudes, evergreen and oak forests flourish in the cooler, but still damp, conditions.

In northern Mexico, vegetation is sparser. The Yucatan Peninsula is covered mostly by a tropical savanna, a treeless grassland. Parts of the Mexican Plateau are covered by desert plants and dry grasslands.

Mexico's mountainous geography makes it a poor candidate for large-scale agriculture. Even so, about 25 percent of the country's people are involved in agriculture in some way. Most of these people are individual farmers who raise small amounts of maize (corn), beans, and squash for their own use. Maize is the country's most important crop. It is used for making tortillas, a staple of the Mexican diet.

In the south coastal areas, where the climate is tropical, farmers raise cacao, tobacco, coffee, pineapples, coconuts, bananas, and other fruits. Cacao is an evergreen plant that grows well in the shade of other trees. Its large seeds are used to make cocoa, cocoa butter, and chocolate. The forests of this region produce rubber, mahogany, and other colorful tropical trees that are sought after by furniture makers.

Along the west coast, irrigated fields are used for growing winter vegetable and fruit crops that are exported to the United States. The northern parts of the country are home to many large cattle ranches, as well as fields of cotton and wheat. People living along the coasts fish for shrimp, sardines, tuna, and mackerel. Because fish makes up only a small part of the Mexican diet, most of the catch is exported.

Mexico's principal export is petroleum, drilled from oil fields along the Gulf coastal plain. The fields, first developed in 1972, make the country the fifth leading exporter of oil. Mexico also exports silver and several other valuable minerals including gold, copper, lead, manganese, zinc, mercury, fluorite, and salt.

Central American Lands

Central America is twelve hundred miles long but only between thirty and three hundred miles wide. At its narrowest point, in Panama, the isthmus is split by the Panama Canal, which links the Atlantic and Pacific Oceans.

The region's landscape is dominated by two features: some of the world's densest rain forests and an eight-hundred-mile-long chain of volcanic mountains that stretches from the Mexican border to central Costa Rica. The islands of the West Indies are actually a series of volcanic mountains once covered by the ocean. Some of the volcanoes, like those in Mexico, are still active.

Tropical vegetation grows in the lowlands and smaller islands of Central America. Above, a tropical beach in St. Kitts and Nevis in the West Indies

Climate in Central America

Like its northern neighbor, Central America has a climate that varies with altitude. The lowland areas along the coast are hot and humid and receive large amounts of rain. Some years more than two hundred inches of rain falls in this area.

Most people live in the cooler highland areas that have a more temperate climate and less rainfall. Temperatures and climates become harsher higher up in the mountains, where snow occasionally falls.

The West Indies and the other Caribbean islands have a tropical climate, with an average annual temperature of 80° F. Rainfall in the region averages between twenty and forty inches, depending on the elevation.

Central American Vegetation and Natural Resources

Because of its varied geography, Central America is home to many different types of vegetation. The lowland rain forests on the eastern half of the country are similar to those in South America, containing many species of trees that are so dense that little light filters through.

On the western side of the country, the lower slopes of the mountains are covered by evergreen forests. Higher up, the forests are similar to those in North America, containing pine and oak trees.

Eruptions from Central America's volcanoes have deposited a layer of ash that has become rich soil, one of the region's greatest natural resources. In this soil coffee bean plants and banana trees thrive, producing the area's primary export crops.

Farmers in the country began growing coffee for export in the early 1800s on the Pacific Coast of Costa Rica and later in the century in El Salvador, Nicaragua, and Guatemala. Bananas were introduced as a crop in 1900 in the tropical coastal lowlands along the Caribbean. Citrus fruits, sugar, cacao, and cotton also grow in abundance in Central American countries.

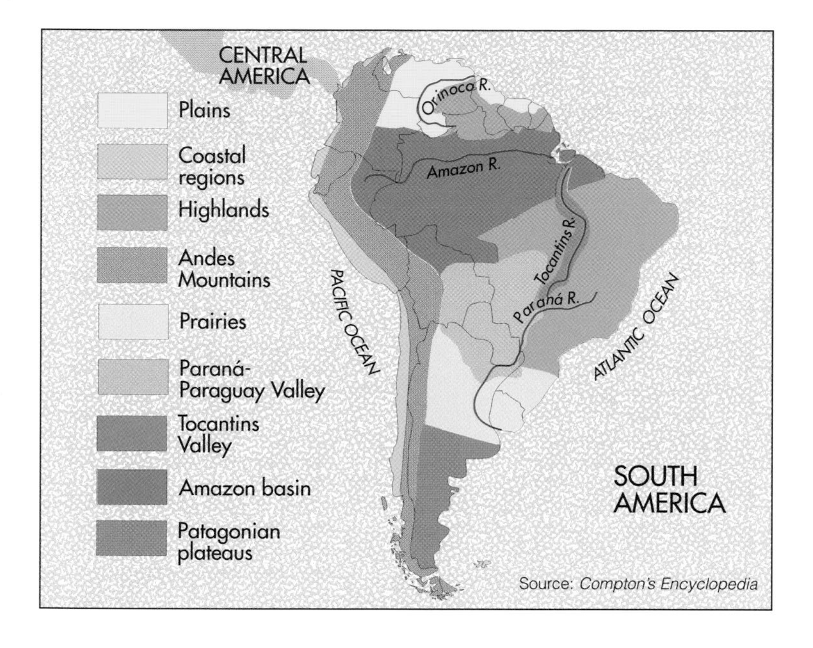

South American Lands

Like Central America, South America is dominated by two aspects of its geography: the soaring spine of the Andes Mountains running along the entire length of the continent's Pacific Coast and the dense jungles of the Amazon rain forest.

In addition, there are several other prominent areas of the continent. Along the eastern side are the highlands of French Guiana and Brazil. In the southern part are the Patagonian plateaus. Between these raised areas are the lowlands of the Orinoco River and Paraguay, in addition to the Amazon basin.

Almost all the rainwater that falls on South America and all its major rivers flow eastward. That is because the chain of Andes Mountains that runs the en-

At right, the Andes Mountains of Peru, where the remains of the Inca city of Machu Picchu,were discovered in 1911.

tire length of the continent's western coast is higher than any other point. A raindrop that falls on the eastern slope of the Andes (if it were not absorbed into the soil) would flow twenty-five hundred miles, eventually landing in the Atlantic Ocean.[4]

Climate of South America

Although the common view of South America is one of a jungle-filled land, it actually has four types of climate. The first is the tropical rain forest. This is found in the Amazon basin (the area around the Amazon River), on part of the Brazilian coast, and on the Pacific coast of Colombia. It is hot and humid. The average temperature is 86° F, and the average rainfall is ninety inches a year. In some parts of Colombia it rains more than three hundred days out of the year, dropping up to 354 inches of water on the lands below.[5]

Around the edges of the rain forest is an area with a climate called tropical savanna. This is a drier climate with little seasonal shift in the temperature. But on most days the temperature ranges from a low of 65°F to a high of 95°F. This type of climate is found in the Orinoco Basin, the Brazilian Highlands, and in western Ecuador.

The southern part of South America has a temperate climate. The temperatures range from 50° F to 77° F, and twelve to twenty-four inches of rain falls each year. This type of climate is found in Paraguay, Bolivia, Brazil, Argentina, and Chile. In southern parts of Chile, glaciers keep the summers cool (below 50° F) and cloudy.

The rest of South America has an arid climate. These areas include the Patagonia region, a narrow strip of land between the Andes Mountains and the Pacific Ocean, northeastern Colombia, and northeastern Brazil. These areas have less than four inches of rain a year and a dry season that may last up to seven months.

South American Vegetation and Natural Resources

South America's vegetation varies according to the climate of a particular region. In the tropical and subtropical climates, rain forests grow massive trees, some more than three hundred feet high. The canopies of the trees are so dense that little light filters through to the forest floor.

These trees are prized for their beautifully colored hardwoods. Mahogany, a particular favorite, is one of the world's densest woods—in fact some logs are so dense they won't even float in water.[6] The rain forests also produce the lightweight balsa tree, from which comes the balsawood found in model airplanes and easily breakable furniture used in movies for action scenes. Rubber trees and cacao are native plants found in the Amazon basin. Rubber trees produce latex, which is used in hundreds of products, from paint to gloves.

Scrub woodlands with smaller trees and less vegetation exist in the drier areas of the tropics. Parts of northeastern Brazil also have dense tangles of thorny bushes. Forests of hardwood trees are found in temperate zones at higher altitudes in southern Brazil and central and southern Chile.

Prairie grasslands grow in the far southern portion of Brazil, the northeastern part of Argentina, and in Uruguay. These lands are most frequently used for cattle grazing.

Arid areas that include land along the Pacific Ocean, parts of Colombia, Venezuela, and Brazil have small desert shrubs, but otherwise there are few plants.

There are more than four billion acres of land in South America, but only a small part of that is good for growing crops. This is partially because the soil is not particularly fertile, despite the continent's image as a lush jungle. The tropical and subtropical rain forests have the poorest soil of all. This is because most nutrients are quickly taken up by the dense vegetation in these areas.[7] Nutrients left over are often washed away by heavy rain.

Agriculture in South America is limited to three areas: the grassland plains in the east, where wheat and corn grow and cattle graze; the temperate parts of the Andes, where farmers produce some crops and raise cattle; and the eastern and southeastern sections of Brazil, where coffee, cacao, and sugarcane grow.

Although South America is not an agricultural powerhouse, it has many other natural resources, including several valuable minerals. Iron ore is found throughout the region, and coal is mined in Colombia, Brazil, Argentina, Peru, Venezuela, and Chile. Venezuela has large pools of petroleum, making that country one of the world's largest petroleum producers. Oil is also found in the countries of Brazil, Ecuador, Peru, and Bolivia.

Gold mining in South America reached a peak in the 1980s when more than five hundred thousand migrant miners searched for the valuable mineral in the Tocantins Valley of Brazil's Amazon region. Brazil's production of gold peaked in 1987 at ninety tons, then declined. Gold mining continues today but not at the levels of the 1980s.

CHAPTER TWO

ADAPTING TO THE ENVIRONMENT

There are hundreds of distinct cultures and lifestyles within the Western Hemisphere. Even within a single nation there may be vast differences in the way people live. Many of these differences are due to the varying ways people have adapted to their physical environment. The type of homes people live in, the clothes they wear, and the kinds of food they grow, harvest, and eat are all influenced in part by the climate and the geography of the land surrounding them.

At left, Ecuadoran children of the Andes. They have adapted their lifestyle to living in the rugged terrain of the Andes.

Canada's People

Despite its large size, much of Canada's population is concentrated in a few areas along its southern border near the United States. Approximately 89 percent of Canada's land is unsettled. Although cities in Canada are as modern and cosmopolitan as those in the

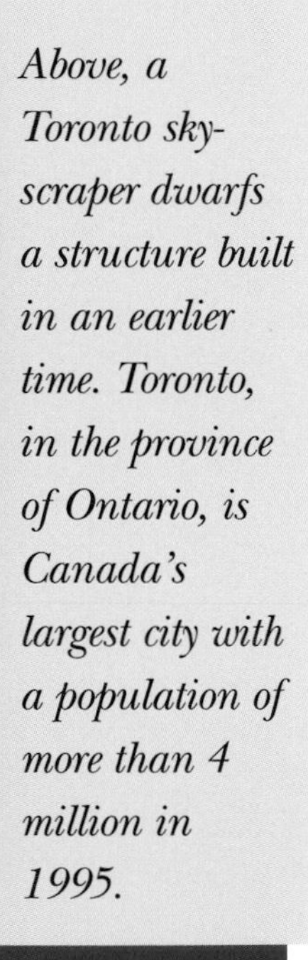

Above, a Toronto skyscraper dwarfs a structure built in an earlier time. Toronto, in the province of Ontario, is Canada's largest city with a population of more than 4 million in 1995.

United States, the wilderness is an integral part of the Canadian culture, even for those living in urban areas. No part of the country is more than sixty miles from the wilderness.[1]

In the eastern part of the country, the Maritime Provinces of New Brunswick, Prince Edward Island, and Nova Scotia are all populated, as is the southern portion of Quebec and the sections on both sides of the St. Lawrence Seaway. Farther west, there are pockets of population in the province of Ontario, mostly around the city of Ottawa, which is Canada's capital, and along the shores of Lake Erie and Lake Ontario.

Most Canadians live in Quebec and Ontario in the areas that border the Great Lakes and the St. Lawrence River. Early settlers sought out the edges where land and water meet, in part because water was the most common source of transportation. Because people wanted access to the water, house lots in Quebec along the coast are long and skinny, with the thin edge of the lot touching the water's edge. This allowed the largest number of people to have a house next to the water.

In the central and western part of the country, people are clustered in the southern portion of Saskatchewan, the southeastern portion of Alberta, and the southwestern portion of Manitoba. People also live in the southern areas of British Columbia, Canada's province on the far western edge of the country. Farther north, where the climate is too cold for large-scale agriculture, only a few pioneer farmers have built homes.

Canadians, like other people in the Western Hemisphere, are shifting toward urban lifestyles and away from rural areas. By the early twentieth century, one-third of Canada's people lived in urban areas. Today, almost three-quarters of the population live in communities of one thousand or more, and half of the population live in cities of one hundred thousand or more.[2] Most of these urban centers are in the south.

Toronto, Canada's largest city, ranks eighteenth among the most populated cities in the Western Hemisphere.[3] More than four million people live there, following an urban lifestyle typical of most cities in the western world.

Life in southern Canada in many ways resembles life in the United States. This is because the two regions share a similar geography and environment. Southern Canadians dress in the same fashions as their U.S. neighbors. Office-filled skyscrapers punctuate city skylines. Houses are a mix of modern structures and older homes built earlier in the century.

Although there are many regional differences in Canadian lifestyles, the biggest difference occurs between the northern and southern parts of the country. While southern Canadians travel a network of modern highways, northerners have few roads and traveling long distances on them in the harsh winter season can be dangerous. There are no paved roads in the Arctic because the region's extreme temperature changes

Life Without Trees

When people in the United States think of a house, they usually think of wood, which is the material most commonly used in homes today and which has been used as a home building material for many years. But in some parts of the Western Hemisphere, there are very few trees or none at all. What do the inhabitants of these areas use to build their homes?

The Inuits of northern Canada live on the tundra, where there are only bushes, moss, and grass. They were among the most creative in their use of alternative materials. In the summer they lived in tents made from a few wooden poles covered by animal hides. In the winter they built shelters from blocks of packed snow. This type of house is called an igloo. Other tribes, who lived along the coast in Alaska, used a combination of earth and driftwood found on the shore. Their kayaks were made from animal skins stretched over a wooden frame. Even their dogsleds could be built without wood—instead they used dried salmon.

The American Indians in the West carved caves from the faces of the cliffs. The early settlers in the Great Plains of the United States sometimes built homes from sod—strips of grassland they cut from the earth and piled row upon row to form walls. Roofs were strips of sod laid on poles and stretched across the walls. A person could be standing on the roof of a settler's house and not even know it was beneath his or her feet.

The Mayans of Central America built their homes from artfully carved stones. These stones were so carefully fitted that many Mayan structures still stand today, despite the many earthquakes in the region.

cause the ground to swell and contract. This action would quickly ruin an asphalt road.

In the winter, many people travel by snowmobile, all-terrain vehicle or sometimes by Bombardier, a large snow-cat-like vehicle with tracks and skis. It is common to see snowmobiles parked outside Arctic homes, just as cars sit in the driveways of homes in southern Canada and the United States.

In the Yukon it can take up to two weeks for a convoy of trucks to travel the 460-mile-long Dempster Highway into the Arctic Circle. These convoys carry bulldozers to clear snowdrifts from their path and special survival gear in case they are slowed by bad weather.[4] Most travel in the north is by airplane. Because there are few airports, many planes use skis for landing on snow in the winter or pontoons for landing on water in the summer.

Children living in northern Canada also face dangers their peers living farther south can only imagine. For instance, students in the Northwest Territories are warned not to feed the polar bears that sometimes wander near their playgrounds. Recess has to be canceled if a bear is spotted nearby.[5]

Climate differences between north and south affect the kinds of homes people build and the clothing they wear. In the Arctic, where winter temperatures can dip below -40°F, warm clothing is a must for survival. Long parkas that hang below the knees are standard outside wear for everyone. Although the Inuits, the native people of the Arctic, often wear synthetic

Above, the city of New York is the largest in the United States and the fifth largest according to population in the world. Only Mexico City in Mexico and São Paulo in Brazil are larger in the Western Hemisphere.

manufactured clothing when in town, they prefer the traditional hand-sewn caribou-skin parkas when they are "out on the land."

Permafrost, the Arctic's frozen land, poses special difficulties for builders. Homes in the Arctic must be built on stilts driven into the permafrost to keep them from melting the land below. If the permafrost were to melt underneath a home, the house would sink into the soil. There are no basements in Arctic homes; in fact, the Inuit language has no word for basement.

Food is more expensive in the Arctic than it is in southern Canada, because it must be brought in by boat or airplane. The short growing season does not allow for much gardening or raising of livestock.

People in the United States

The United States has a population that is spaced fairly evenly throughout the country rather than being crowded together in just a few areas. This is because a moderate climate allows people to live in almost every area of the country; people of one region are not separated from those of another by large areas of uninhabitable land as in Canada.

The widespread settling was also helped by the construction of railroads in the mid-1800s, which moved thousands of people from the eastern part of the country to the west.

Today, the most heavily populated areas in the United States are along the eastern seaboard, the southwestern coast, and in areas around the Great Lakes along the northern border of the country.

U.S. Lifestyle

In the United States, as elsewhere, people have learned to adapt to their environment. In New England, for example, farmers made good use of the rocks left in fields by ancient glaciers. After wresting these obstacles from the ground in order to plant their crops, the inventive farmers piled the rocks in rows to form walls that kept their livestock from wandering and marked the boundaries of their land. To this day, the stone wall is an enduring symbol of New England.

The regional differences in lifestyle in the United States are not as sharply defined as they are in Canada. The regions do have subtle differences, however, many of which are the result of climate.

In parts of the country where winters are cold and snowy—the Northeast and northern Midwest—recreational activities focus on skiing, snowmobiling, ice fishing, and sledding. These areas also enjoy a summer season, but it is often only a few months long.

People who live in these colder regions prepare well for winter. They own warm clothing and boots. Their cars have special tires designed to grip the road through a layer of snow. Some cars have special devices designed to preheat the engine to make it easier to start on cold mornings. Every town and city has a fleet of snowplows to clear roads after winter storms.

Above, a child in the cold Northeast takes advantage of the snow to have some fun.

The houses of these regions also reflect the cold climate. Homes in the Northeast and northern Midwest have steeply sloped roofs that allow snow to slide off without damaging the structure. Homes in these areas also have heavy-duty furnaces or boilers that burn oil or natural gas to provide heat in the winter.

Until recently, many New England homes were saltboxes, a type of house with a steeply pitched roof and small windows. These features were designed to trap as much heat as possible.[6] Today, modern building materials and furnaces allow builders to use larger windows, even in the cold Northeast.

People in the South and Southwest, where summer temperatures frequently climb into the 90s, take steps to protect themselves from the sun and heat. Darkly tinted automobile windows help keep riders cool. Homes may have flatter roofs because there is no snow. Most homes and automobiles have air-conditioning.

Before the days of electricity, homes were built to take advantage of natural cooling breezes, with large windows and open spaces inside for good air circulation. Homes had wooden shutters that could be closed during the hot part of the day, to keep the sun out. The wide porches found on many southern homes allowed people to gather outside where it was cooler.

The heat, perhaps the South's most prominent environmental characteristic, has also influenced the way people live. Two southern writers, William A. Bake and James J. Kilpatrick, note that the tendency of southerners to gather frequently may be because the weather does not form a barrier to traveling.[7] The same writers also note that life is slower in the South, probably because of the warm weather.[8]

Mexico's People

Most of Mexico's people live in the south-central part of the country at elevations above 3,280 feet, where the climate is cooler and less humid. The country's inhabitants have always centered in this area, even before the arrival of the Europeans.

Much of Mexico's population today is concentrated in urban areas. Unable to make a living from farming, poor peasants poured into cities looking for work. As a result, Mexico City has almost five times as many people as in 1963, when the population was less than five million. By the year 2000, the city is expected to become the most populous in the world, with an estimated thirty million people.[9]

The lives of urban middle-class Mexicans are much the same as those of other North American city dwellers. Above, members of Mexico's stock exchange

Mexican Lifestyle

The Mexican lifestyle varies greatly from city to rural areas. Rich and middle-class people who dwell in the city live in modern apartment buildings made of concrete or steel with air-conditioning, electricity, and modern plumbing. Their lifestyles are in many ways similar to those of people living in the United States and Canada. Urban areas and some of the Mexican countryside are served by a network of modern roads and highways. Poorer people in urban areas live in houses made from concrete blocks with tin roofs.

People in rural areas lead lives more similar to those of the original inhabitants. Their homes are often constructed from adobe, a building material made from clay mixed with straw that helps keep the inside of the house cool. The roofs of the buildings are made from thatch, bundles of straw tied onto a framework of poles. Other homes are made from bamboo or poles tied together. These homes have dirt floors, where the occupants sleep on mats made from woven grasses.

People in rural Mexico till their fields, if they have any, using oxen or horses. If they sell their produce at the market, they must carry it there using burros or, perhaps, their own backs.

One way Mexicans have adapted to their warm climate is by resting during the middle of the day, when the sun is hottest. They return to work later in the day when it is cooler. This resting period is called a siesta and is found throughout the Latin American culture.

Central America's People

Like their Mexican neighbors, the majority of Central Americans live at altitudes between three thousand to eight thousand feet to take advantage of the cooler, more moderate climate found at that height.

More than half of the people live in the country, earning their living by growing corn, beans, and other vegetables, which they use for their own consumption and may also sell at local markets. The concentration of people in the rural areas of the highlands, however, puts an increased strain on the resources in a relatively small area. This is true in areas of western Guatemala, much of El Salvador, central Costa Rica, and the Nicaraguan lake region. Many people in these areas are moving to urban centers in search of work.

The eastern half of the region, the Caribbean lowlands, is virtually uninhabited because of high heat and disease-spreading mosquitoes.

The photos above show different ways people in Panama adapted the environment to their needs. Above, an abode villa with clay-tiled roof. Below, a grass hut.

Central American Lifestyle

In Central America, as in the rest of Latin America, lifestyles vary widely between urban and rural areas. Housing in Central America reflects these differences and illustrates how people use the material at hand to provide shelter for themselves. Modern materials like concrete and steel are used to construct many buildings in the region's cities. On the fringes of the urban areas, people live in shacks made from a combination of concrete blocks, wooden boards, and tin roofs.

Most buildings in Central America are not tall. This is to help keep them stable during the frequent earthquakes that shake this part of the hemisphere.

Many of the Indians in Central America live as their Mayan ancestors did, seeking shelter in adobe huts with thatched roofs and dirt floors. The thick mud walls help keep the inside cool. Reeds from marshes may also be used for home construction in the lowland areas. These families live in the country and grow corn, black beans, and squash for their own consumption. Some also raise a few small animals, such as goats, for milk and meat.

Wealthy landowners in the country may have villas. While the walls of these fancy houses may be made from the same adobe bricks used by poor peasants, they are painted and have all of the amenities of modern homes. The roofs on these buildings are often made from red clay tiles.

South America's People

South America's rugged mountains, deserts, jungles, and rivers have divided its people into separate clusters, some of whom have little contact with one another. Except for small tribes of Indians in the interior of the rain forest and some farmers and ranchers on the plains, most South Americans live along the fringes of the continent, near the coasts. Even along the coasts, however, the people have gathered in irregular clusters around urban centers.

South American Lifestyle

Living styles in South America vary as widely as its geography. Some Indian tribes, separated from twentieth century technology by dense forests and jungle, continue to live much as their ancestors did hundreds of years ago. For example, an Indian family in the hot, humid Amazon jungle of Brazil lives in a hut of mud bricks and a wooden roof. They sleep in hammocks hung from the ceiling. There are windows in the house, but they are not covered by glass because of the warm climate. Family members grow all the food they need by clearing part of the rain forest around their home. Members of the family also hunt for fish or alligators in the river, using a bow and arrows or spears.

A typical family on the high plains of the Andes Mountains in Bolivia may make a living by growing and selling potatoes, one of the few vegetables that grow well in the stony soil of the region. Their house is made of concrete and stone with a metal roof.

Most South Americans, however, live in or around urban centers. Six of the ten largest cities in the Western Hemisphere are located in South America.[10] Life for the rich and middle class in South American cities is much like that in other cities in the hemisphere. Members of the middle and upper classes live in apartment buildings with electricity and modern conveniences. Urban communities have schools, newspapers, television stations, paved roads, automobiles, and traffic jams, just as their northern neighbors.

But the urban poor face a constant struggle to survive. One-sixth of the people in São Paulo and Rio de Janeiro in Brazil live in slums circling the city.[11] Their homes are made from rags, cardboard, sheet metal, or wood scraps. They have no plumbing or electricity. The poor in cities in Chile, Ecuador, and Peru live under similar conditions.

CHAPTER THREE

SHAPING THE ENVIRONMENT

The first settlers of the Western Hemisphere, the people now called Native Americans, believed they were a small part of a larger whole. Their lives were attuned to the rhythm of the environment. Many of the early people of the Americas were nomadic hunters and gatherers. They followed migrating herds of caribou or bison and harvested berries and fruits that grew naturally in the areas where they lived. Everything they owned could be carried with them.[1] They adapted their lives to the conditions imposed on them by nature. Only a few, such as the Mayans of Mexico and Central America and the Incas of South America, built permanent structures.

The European explorers and settlers brought a different way of relating to the environment when they arrived in the 1500s. They quickly created an environment similar to the one they had left behind, building

At left, a giant machine loads massive logs. Machines have played a major role in helping people shape and use the environment.

villages and roads in their new homeland. They cleared forests to make way for fields that could be used to raise crops or graze cattle. Unlike the Native Americans who adjusted their lives to the environment, the Europeans shaped the environment to meet their needs.

For example, the settlers brought with them the technology to harness the power of moving water. By building dams and waterwheels, they turned the force of a stream into power for machinery that ground wheat into flour and that later produced manufactured goods.

These deliberate changes allowed the new settlers to flourish and enjoy a style of living far higher than that of the land's original inhabitants. The Europeans, who set up permanent homes and whose farms produced an abundant food supply, soon outnumbered the native people. Before the first Europeans landed in the Western Hemisphere in the 1500s, between sixty million and ninety million people lived on the two continents.[2] Since that time, the population has grown to more than 708 million people in the early 1990s and continues to increase every day.[3]

This enormous growth meant that more of the earth's resources had to be converted for human use: to produce food, to make room for houses and roads, and to create more energy.

But these uses of the earth's resources have had many negative side effects, some of which we are only beginning to understand.

At left, a tract of forest that has been cleared by North American loggers

Agriculture, Grazing, and Forestry

Throughout the Western Hemisphere, humans have shaped and modified the land to make it suitable for agriculture. In the United States and Canada, modern farmers using massive tractors have plowed under much of the native prairie grasses in their country's interior sections.

In place of the grasses, farmers have planted vast fields of corn, wheat, and soybeans. Modifying the land this way allows a few farmers to raise large amounts of food that can feed millions of people.

Grasslands in more arid climates have been taken over by cattle ranchers for grazing.

When Europeans arrived in the Western Hemisphere, great tracts of forest covered North America. One estimate is that 950 million acres of forest covered the United States when the Pilgrims arrived from England in the 1600s. By 1920, one-third of that forest had vanished, cut down to make room for fields, towns, and roads.[4] Today, less than 5 percent of that original forest is still standing.[5] Vast tracts of North American forests were also chopped down for lumber to make houses or turned into pulp for paper.

Above, a forest that was burned to create ash to fertilize the soil. The practice is called slash and burn agriculture.

In Central and South America, farmers, called *campesinos,* cut thousands of acres of rain forest trees every year to create open areas for their crops. After cutting the trees, the farmers burn them and use the ash to help fertilize the soil. This is called slash and burn agriculture; this method is also used in parts of North America. In the late 1980s there were so many of these fires that enormous clouds of smoke hid parts of the South American jungle for days. The smoke was so thick it could be seen by astronauts orbiting the earth in the space shuttle.[6]

The soil of the South American rain forest is not nearly as rich as that of the plains of the United States and Canada. After only a few years of cultivation, the soil in the rain forest can no longer support crops. Farmers are forced to move on to a new patch of forest and repeat the pattern.[7] The rain forests have also been cut heavily to make room for coffee, tea, bananas, and other crops grown for export.

Central and South American government leaders provided incentives to ranchers to raise cattle because they thought there was an enormous market for cheap beef in the United States. The incentives, offered as a way to boost the economy of the region, encouraged ranchers to destroy large tracts of rain forest to create grazing lands.

But the returns from this policy have not lived up to the hopes of the governments. A study by John Browder, professor of urban planning at Virginia Polytechnic Institute and State University, showed that the average ranch in Brazil repays only one-quarter of the money spent to raise the beef.[8]

Transportation

One of humanity's greatest achievements, and one that has had a huge impact on the environment, is the development of fast, efficient transportation. A five-hundred-mile journey that might have taken the Western Hemisphere's early inhabitants weeks to complete on foot now takes eight to ten hours by car, even less by air.

The transportation network in the Western Hemisphere began with dirt tracks on which horses and buggies rode. Later came trains, riding on shiny steel rails, followed by the automobile. Today, paved roads cover almost all the United States and southern Canada. Large parts of Mexico also have modern highways.

Paved roads in Central and South America are rare outside urban areas. But dirt roads lead into the wilderness, bringing development with them.

Two massive highways travel through the wilds of the Western Hemisphere. The fifteen-hundred-mile-long Alaskan Highway connects the Canadian province of British Columbia with Alaska. The Pan American Highway, which is complete except for a sixty-mile gap in a swampy, mountainous region between Panama and Colombia, stretches sixteen thousand miles from the U.S.-Canadian border south through Central and South America to Santiago, Chile.

The rapid development of transportation has allowed humans to spread throughout the Western Hemisphere—and also to increase their impact upon the land. The development of the railroad aided the westward expansion of the United States, bringing thousands of people to areas that were once wilderness. Road construction in South America has had a similar effect, bringing people and development to once untouched sections of the rain forest.

The need for efficient, fast transportation has also transformed the hemisphere's waterways. The Mississippi River, in the middle of the United States, carries hundreds of barges every day. Oceangoing vessels travel from the Atlantic Ocean up the Amazon River, bringing supplies to people living in the jungle and carrying goods out.

In some cases humans have created bodies of water where there was once dry land, in order to travel from one point to another. Many of these man-made bodies of water, called canals, were built in the eastern part of the United States in the early nineteenth century. One of the best known is the 363-mile-long Erie Canal, which was completed in 1825 and connected the Hud-

A ship passes through the Panama Canal. Ships passing through the 51-mile-long canal are lifted 85 feet above sea level.

son River (and thereby New York City) with Lake Erie. That canal is still used today by freight ships.

Another well-known canal is the 51-mile-long Panama Canal, which crosses a narrow stretch of the Central American country of Panama and connects the Atlantic and Pacific Oceans. For large ships it is the fastest way to get from one coast of the Western Hemisphere to the other. Without the canal, ships would have to travel another ten thousand nautical miles around the southern tip of South America. At the time of its completion in 1914, the Panama Canal was considered the greatest engineering feat of its time.[9]

Water Control

The relationship between humans and nature is often compared to a battle. This struggle is particularly fierce along the shore, where the land meets the water. Here, people build their homes as close as they can to the water, sometimes right on the beach. But when homes are built too close to the shoreline, storms, unusually high tides, and unsteady sands can quickly turn an expensive beach house into a pile of sticks or an entire village into a ghost town.

In an attempt to protect man-made property, engineers build stone and concrete seawalls to block ocean surges. In some coastal areas these walls extend for miles along the beach. Sometimes, seaside communities must move sand from other areas onto the beach to replace sand eroded by the action of the ocean.

Builders also reshape coastlines when they fill marshlands, which are often found in the areas between dry land and water. Until recent laws put limits on the practice, contractors filled wetlands with soil or built canals to divert the water to other areas so the land could be used for houses or shopping malls.

Like those who settle along the coast, people who live next to rivers have for years tried to control the changing flow of water in an effort to prevent it from flooding their homes. Dams are one device used to help control floods by holding back sudden surges in water that occur after a rainstorm. After the storm has passed, dam operators slowly release the stored water.

Another flood control device is a levee. This is a wall, usually built from sand, that is erected alongside a river. It elevates the riverbank so that when the river rises after a rainstorm, it won't overflow and cause a flood. Levees are built along the sides of rivers where they pass through cities and fields. This allows humans to build homes and roads and grow crops in areas that otherwise would be too wet.

Search for Energy

Modern civilization's demand for energy has produced some of the most serious damage to the environments of the Western Hemisphere. Pre-European populations had little need for outside energy sources. These people built small wood or coal fires for cooking and warmth. Some Indian tribes used animal fat to fuel stoves for cooking or lanterns for light. Their bodies were more accustomed to conditions in the outdoors than those of the European settlers. When the weather turned cold, the native people wore more clothing. When they had to travel, they walked.

People today require vast amounts of energy to control the temperature inside offices and homes, provide transportation, communicate with each other, and operate machinery. Practically every facet of modern life revolves around equipment and appliances that require some form of energy to run.

Fossil fuels—substances like petroleum and coal—provide much of the energy modern life requires. The search for coal made massive changes in Western Hemisphere lands, leaving huge, gaping holes in the landscape. Until the early 1900s, most coal was dug

Above, a mountain in Idaho shows the effects of strip-mining for gold.

from underground mines. With the invention of the steam shovel, miners began to strip-mine coal from the surface. In this method, giant pieces of machinery strip soil and vegetation from the surface and dig down until a seam of coal is found. Then the machinery removes the coal.

For many years, strip-mined land was left in this barren state. In 1977 the U.S. Congress passed a law requiring the land to be rebuilt using the soil that was originally removed. Despite this law, many old mining sites remain damaged. Another kind of strip-mining is used when the coal is in a hill or mountainside. The machinery is used to shave away the mountain, in some cases reducing it to level ground. Similar mining techniques are used to remove other minerals from the ground, including gold, iron, and copper.

Petroleum

The search for petroleum makes less of a mark on the surface of the earth because the liquid is pumped up from vast underground pools. The only machinery that shows aboveground is the drilling rig.

But oil production has had a disastrous effect on the environment in cases where the oil spills while being transported from the well to a refinery. These spills are especially bad for the environment when they happen at sea near shore. An oil spill in the ocean can kill vast numbers of marine organisms. In 1989 a tanker in Alaska named the *Exxon Valdez* struck a rock near the shore. More than 250,000 barrels of oil leaked from the ship's ruptured hull and spread out into Prince William Sound. Eventually much of the oil washed up on shore. Hundreds of marine mammals and seabirds were killed, as well as smaller animals.[10]

Hydropower

The early settlers of the Western Hemisphere brought with them the technology to get energy from falling water—the water wheel. These wheels were moved by the force of water falling from one level to another, usually over a man-made dam built across a stream or river. The moving wheel was used to power machinery that cut wood, ground grain, or performed other manufacturing tasks.

Over time people developed this technology to a larger scale. Today, massive dams block rivers throughout the Western Hemisphere. The water trapped behind these structures—which are called hydroelectric projects—is used to create electricity. The force of the water, as it is released, turns a system of wheels or paddles called turbines. The electricity produced by the turning wheels is used to power the surrounding cities and towns.

In some cases, hydroelectric projects have completely changed the landscape, covering land that was once forests and fields and deserts. In the United States, construction of the Hoover Dam on the Colorado River in 1936 created the 115-mile-long Mead Lake in an area that was once a desert. In addition to the energy provided by the dam, the stored water irri-

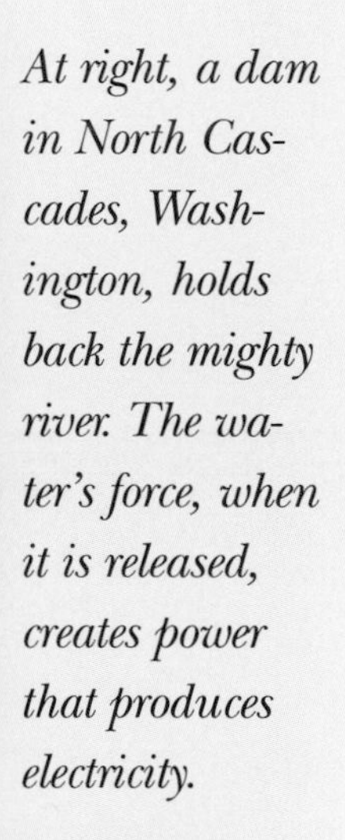

At right, a dam in North Cascades, Washington, holds back the mighty river. The water's force, when it is released, creates power that produces electricity.

gates crops that would otherwise never grow in the region's arid climate. Canals divert the water from the dam and carry it to hundreds of thousands of acres in the surrounding desert. The system also supplies water to the valleys of southern California and to Arizona.

In the Western Hemisphere, Canada is the leading generator of hydroelectric power, followed by the United States and Brazil, which built the enormous Itaipu Dam on the Paraná River.

Nuclear power

Nuclear power was once thought to be an almost magical source of energy. In the 1940s scientists discovered they could create massive amounts of energy by splitting uranium atoms. This process is called nuclear fission. A small amount of uranium, a mineral mined from the soil, can produce enough power to supply entire cities.

Soon nuclear power plants were built in Canada and the United States. These plants used the energy released by nuclear fission to heat water into steam. The steam drove turbines that produced electricity. At first it seemed that this might solve the energy problems of the modern world. This process didn't pollute the air or the water—providing the plant didn't leak or explode—and there were no concerns about uranium shortages.

But nuclear power has created serious concerns. When the uranium atom is split, it produces two kinds of energy: heat and radiation. The radiation is deadly to living creatures, and so the entire fission process must take place in a specially designed building made of lead and concrete that prevents the radiation from escaping into the atmosphere.

Another danger occurs after the uranium used to power the nuclear plant is exhausted. Even though it can no longer provide heat energy, the used uranium remains radioactive and is dangerous for as long as ten thousand years. It must be disposed of in a special and very expensive manner, buried deep in the earth or stored temporarily in reinforced containers. Scientists have not yet discovered a way to dispose of the used nuclear material that is guaranteed to be safe.

Above, steam escapes from a U.S. nuclear power plant. The plant produces inexpensive electricity without polluting the atmosphere, but scientists worry about what to do with the radioactive waste created by the plant.

CHAPTER FOUR

PAYING THE BILL

In the past century, we have made great strides in technology, increasing our ability to alter the environment to our needs. This has helped to make life better for many people. Homes are warm, food plentiful, transportation easy and fast.

These advances, however, haven't come without consequences. Sometimes the results are easy to predict. For instance, constructing a road or a house damages the land on which it sits; a shopping center alters the landscape where it is built.

Sometimes the effects are not so easy to see—at least at first. People didn't notice that the burning of fossil fuels was slowly polluting the air and possibly raising the temperature of the planet. Using certain chemicals has damaged a protective part of our atmosphere and left us with a greater risk of some cancers. Roads and parking lots cover land that once absorbed rain. The rain now flows into rivers that flood from the extra volume of water.

People are beginning to realize that their activities have a bigger impact than they once thought. They are

At left, workers try to clean up the beach after an oil spill along the Oregon coast.

also learning how the different parts of the environment are connected. They are beginning to see that affecting one part can start a chain reaction that spreads throughout a region, even throughout the planet.

WATER EVERYWHERE, AND NOT A DROP TO DRINK

Above, untreated sewage pours into a stream. Such pollution has contaminated water throughout the Western Hemisphere.

Clean water is a necessity of life. Without it the human race, as well as all life on earth, would vanish. Yet, until recently, many people took water for granted.

Until the middle part of this century, humans regularly used rivers as a cheap form of waste disposal. The people of cities piped their sewage directly into rivers, which carried it away. Large manufacturing plants dumped chemical waste into the rivers. Sometimes the rivers became so polluted they turned different colors. One river, the Cuyahoga near Cleveland, Ohio, caught fire in the summer of 1969 because it was so polluted.[1]

Water pollution is a major problem in many parts of Central and South America, where governments have little money to pay for treating sewage and chemical waste. The Choqueyapu River, which runs through Bolivia, is used as an open sewer by that country's capital city, La Paz. Health officials in Bolivia say residents of the city and of rural areas downstream are in danger of getting sick from drinking the river water.[2]

Oil spills

It can be particularly difficult to clean water and

wetlands polluted by some oil spills. For instance, in 1986, an oil storage tank near Colon, Panama, ruptured, spilling about one hundred thousand barrels of crude oil. Much of the oil was washed into a mangrove swamp, where it eventually settled and was absorbed into the sediment. Because of the environment, the oil has been slow to break down and continues to surface each year during spring floods.[3] On the other hand, the habitat of Prince William Sound, the site of the *Exxon Valdez* accident in 1989, appears to have returned to normal due to the weather and a massive cleanup effort.[4]

Flooding

Humans have created other problems by constructing roads and buildings where marshes once thrived. This can lead to flooding. Rivers use wetland areas to control the flow of water. When a river rises after a storm, the extra water flows into these wetlands, which absorb the water. When the river falls back to its normal level, the water flows out of the wetlands and back into the river.

In some areas the wetlands have been replaced with levees and other man-made flood control devices. These devices block the natural interaction between river and wetlands. Instead of spreading out slowly, the river is forced to rise higher between the walls of the levee. If the levee holds, everything is fine. But if the levee breaks or overflows, the land on the other side of the river is flooded.

Loss of wetlands in the U.S. Midwest contributed to floods that devastated the area in 1993. Before the floods, Illinois had lost 85 percent of its wetlands; Missouri had lost 87 percent, and Iowa 90 percent.

—1995 Information Please Almanac

When rivers overflow their banks, the results can damage homes and destroy crops. At right, the rising Saco River in Maine floods a home.

Flooding has a two-part effect on agriculture. The initial damage is caused by the flood itself, covering growing plants in the fields and suffocating them. In addition, floodwaters bring large amounts of silt and sand with them, depositing them on fields. Once the floodwaters have receded, the sand (which can be several feet thick) must be pushed aside by bulldozers before the field can be planted again. Sometimes, instead of carrying sand into a field, floodwaters will actually scour topsoil from the land, leaving behind rocky, infertile soil.

All of this, however, is not necessarily permanent. According to an article written in 1994, farmers in the Midwest reaped record harvests a year after their fields

The Flood of 1997

In the spring of 1997, nature proved again that no matter how technologically advanced our defenses are, we still have to pay the price when we ignore natural forces. In mid-April, following an unusually hard winter, water from melting snow filled the Red River to overflowing. The floodwaters submerged about 4.5 million acres of land, including several towns, in North Dakota and Minnesota. Damage caused by the flood was estimated to be in the billions of dollars.

One of the hardest hit towns was Grand Forks, North Dakota. Not only did floodwaters cover most of the town, forcing the evacuation of fifty thousand people; they also set off a fire that destroyed much of the town's business district. The floodwater was so deep that firefighters could not reach the burning buildings to extinguish the blaze.

According to the National Weather Service and experts from North Dakota State University, the flood was made worse by a combination of man-made projects and natural forces. Levees built to protect towns from floods speeded the river's flow and caused more flooding in areas without levees. Heavier than usual snowfalls and ice jams that prevented rivers from draining also made the flood worse. Despite flooding in the past, people continue to build in the area's sloping valleys and on flat plains along the Red River. The lay of the land directed water into massive pools in the valleys. Along the flat plains, the water spread over a large area, forcing one hundred thousand people from their homes.

"Mother Nature will find a way over, under or around anything you put in its path," a National Weather Service official said.

—*Newsweek*, May 5, 1997

Air pollution is so severe in Mexico City, pictured above, that many of its residents suffer from lung diseases.

had been covered by several feet of water. The article noted that the farmers had cleared their fields of debris and had been blessed that summer with sunny and relatively dry weather.[5]

Air pollution/Smog

The discovery of fossil fuels has helped people take great leaps forward in development. But it has also created a problem that threatens the lives of many people—air pollution.

The burning of fossil fuels, such as gasoline in a car or coal and oil in an industrial plant, releases many different chemicals into the air. These chemicals include compounds called hydrocarbons and nitrogen oxides.

When these chemicals interact with sunlight they create a type of air pollution called ground-level ozone, or smog. The California city of Los Angeles, which has millions of cars, has become famous for its smog, which reduces visibility and makes it difficult for some people to breathe. Sometimes smog levels are so high that doctors tell sick people not to go outside because it can damage their lungs. It also causes headaches, burning eyes, and diseases in young children.[6]

This kind of pollution is most common over large cities or industrial areas, where many fossil fuels are burned. It is especially bad in cities in Mexico and South America, where government pollution regulations are not as strict as those in the United States and Canada. In Mexico City, air pollution is such a severe problem that many of its residents have respiratory disease. This is because the city is home to many industries and millions of cars and trucks. Some have said breathing the air in this Mexican city is like smoking two packs of cigarettes a day.[7]

Pollution created in the city can become a problem in areas that are far away. Less populated areas in the northeastern United States have been plagued by ground level ozone that scientists believe is created from automobile and industrial emissions produced farther south. Wind currents moving north along the coast carry pollution from large cities of the Mid-Atlantic states to the Northeast, where sunlight turns the pollution into ozone.

Tiny particles of soot are also released when fossil

fuels are burned. Like smog, these sulfates and other soot particles have been linked to health problems, especially among children. It is estimated that as many as fifty thousand people die each year in the United States and Canada because of the airborne particles.[8]

Rain that Kills

Burning fossil fuels in power plants and huge factories leads to another type of pollution called acid rain. Sulfur oxides and nitrous oxides are released into the air when fossil fuels are burned. These compounds turn into acids, the same kinds of acids found in a chemistry set. When it rains, these acids fall to earth and dissolve in the rainwater, which flows into lakes and rivers. The acid rain kills fish and other forms of marine life. When all the living creatures in a body of water are gone, that water is said to be dead.

In the Western Hemisphere, acid rain is a problem only in North America, in the northeastern part of the United States and in eastern parts of Canada. It has not yet been reported to be a problem in Central and South America.

In the United States, hundreds of lakes in the northeastern part of the country are considered dead from acid rain. In addition to poisoning lakes, acid rain kills trees by damaging the soil in which the trees grow. It also damages human creations. Statues and buildings made of stone are slowly eroded every year by acid rain. It damages the paint on cars as well.

Like other forms of air pollution, acid rain can cause problems hundreds of miles away from the smokestack where it was created. This has caused friction between the United States and Canada. Thousands of square miles of forests in eastern Canada are threatened by acid rain.[9] The Canadian government claims the pollution that causes the rain comes from the smokestacks of power plants in the United States. The United States denies it is causing Canada's acid rain problem.

Global Warming

During the summer of 1988, temperatures across the United States soared to unusually high levels. At the same time, parts of the country were gripped by a serious drought. People began to wonder if this was the beginning of something scientists had been talking about for several years—global warming.

Scientists know certain gases in the earth's atmosphere, such as carbon dioxide and methane, trap heat from the sun by preventing it from leaving the atmosphere. This is the same way a greenhouse heats itself. Because of this, these gases are known as greenhouse gases.

Greenhouse gases include carbon dioxide, methane, nitrous oxide, and water vapor. All of these gases are produced by burning fossil and other fuels. They are also produced by decaying matter, such as garbage in landfills.

Above, pollution spews from a chemical plant's smokestack. Some scientists predict that greenhouse gases will raise the earth's temperature by 9° F within the next one hundred years.

—1995 Information Please Almanac

Global warming is made worse by the burning of rain forests of the Western Hemisphere. Burning trees release carbon dioxide into the atmosphere. Even worse, trees that are burned cannot help remove carbon dioxide from the atmosphere. Trees and other green plants use carbon dioxide and sunlight to create energy for themselves.

As these gases collect in the atmosphere, scientists believe they will cause the earth to become warmer by trapping greater amounts of the sun's energy. Researchers studying the earth's atmosphere have recorded increases in the amount of greenhouse gases there. They say that the amounts have been rising since the beginning of the industrial revolution in the nineteenth century.

If the earth's temperature increases enough, some scientists are predicting far worse catastrophes than a few hot summers. Polar ice caps could melt, causing the oceans to rise and flood coastal cities. Sea levels have already risen, causing some beaches on the eastern shore of the United States to shrink. Scientists who study the coastlines say global warming could be to blame, although they are not certain.[10]

Global warming could also cause changes in weather and climate. Areas where large amounts of grain are raised could become deserts. Warmer weather would create terrible hurricanes and tornadoes, causing immense amounts of damage to property and the deaths of many people.

Scientists are divided on whether the earth is actually warming. But many say if we wait for more proof, it may be too late to stop the warming trend.

Deforestation and Species Loss

The early European settlers in the Western Hemisphere saw forests as a source for material, such as firewood, lumber for homes, and pulp for paper. They also saw the thick woods as a nuisance, covering land that could be better used for agriculture, cattle grazing, or human habitation. They cut the trees and cleared the forests that surrounded them, a process called deforestation.

Today, the largest surviving forests in North America—in the northern part of the United States and Canada—face the threat of overcutting by paper and lumber companies. Some environmentalists fear that if logging is not reduced, these forests may someday disappear.

The rain forests of Central and South America face a similar threat from ranchers and farmers, who clear the area for crops and grazing. Almost all the forests of western Ecuador, El Salvador, and Haiti have been destroyed; logging and farming have claimed much of the forests of southern Brazil.[11]

The loss of a forest has many negative effects that spread far beyond the forest itself. It destroys the home of many plants and animals that depend on the forest for life. Scientists estimate that more than one hundred plant and animal species become extinct every day. A large majority of these species—as much as 80 percent—live in tropical rain forests.

Many of these plants and animals have not yet been discovered by humans.[12] University of Pennsylvania biologist Daniel Janzen has compared the destruction of rain forests and the life in them to burning a library without knowing what books were inside.[13]

The loss of Central and South American rain forests may be affecting life in the United States and Canada. Biologists have reported that many songbirds found in North America have disappeared in recent years. They believe that one cause may be the destruction of the rain forests, where many songbirds spend the winter. Birds without a place to live during the cold winter months die.

The loss of species may also have a serious effect on humans. People who develop drugs note that many compounds are discovered in plants that live in rain forests. Many other useful plants may be growing in the forests that could be used for cures to some of humanity's worst diseases, including cancer and AIDS. But these plants may never be discovered if the forest in which they live is destroyed.

Fish and other species are at risk from overharvesting. Some species of whales are nearing extinction because too many have been killed before they could reproduce. One-third of North America's freshwater fish are now rare or threatened with extinction. In the United States, one-third of the fish in coastal waters have continued to decrease in number since 1975.[14]

Where Did the Cod Go?

Ever since the first European set foot on the rocky, barren shores of Newfoundland and saw the waters teeming with fish, the Canadian island has been known for one thing: cod.

For hundreds of years, the inhabitants of Newfoundland have been either fishermen or involved in the business of fishing. For many, it seemed as though that was the way life would be forever.

But in the late 1980s and early 1990s the cod began disappearing. Fishermen returned from long days at sea with smaller and smaller catches. Scientists said the cod population was on the verge of collapse because it had been overfished.

To prevent a complete disaster, the Canadian government in 1995 told fishermen they had to stop catching cod. The government and scientists hoped that during the break in fishing, the cod population would grow again.

But the order threw more than twenty-seven thousand fishermen out of work. It also ended work for many people involved in other parts of the fishing industry, including those who processed and packed fish.

By 1997 the government of Canada had begun to allow a few fishermen to catch a limited number of cod. But the total amount of the year's catch was less than one fifth of what the fishermen had caught in earlier years. Many fisherman had decided to give up fishing altogether and had left the island to look for work elsewhere.

The number of American oysters in Chesapeake Bay has declined by 99 percent since 1870. The crustaceans once filtered the water in the bay every three days, helping keep it clear. Today the bay is muddy in part because of the decline in oysters.[15]

Other fisheries that have suffered because of overharvesting include cod and herring in the Atlantic Ocean, perch and king crab in the Pacific Ocean, and Peruvian anchovies.

Erosion and Soil Damage

The destruction of forests has another negative side effect: erosion. Erosion is caused by wind blowing or water running over bare soil. Pieces of the soil are picked up and carried along. Eventually the soil is dropped somewhere else—a stream, a river, a lake, or the ocean. Glaciers also play a part in causing erosion by scraping away top soil, trees, and other vegetation.

The action of erosion moves the soil from a place where it belongs—on the ground where it contains nutrients needed by growing plants—to a place where it doesn't—a body of water.

Erosion happens naturally across the entire Western Hemisphere. It is made worse when large tracts of forest land are cut. It is especially bad in the rain forests of South America because of the large volume of rain that falls there. As raindrops fall in a rain forest, the leaves of the trees help to slow the speed of the rain. By the time the raindrop strikes the ground, it is

The photo at left shows the effects of erosion along the unprotected coastline.

traveling slowly enough that it can be absorbed into the soil. Once the raindrop is absorbed into the soil, it is gathered by the roots of the trees.

If there are no trees, raindrops strike the ground with extra force. Instead of being absorbed into the ground, the rain flows away, carrying pieces of soil with it. Even if the raindrop is absorbed, there are no tree roots to gather it. The ground becomes soaked and muddy. If this happens on a steep hillside, large sections of the earth can actually slide away. This is called a mudslide, a frequent occurrence in hilly or mountainous areas where many of the trees have been cut.

In places as diverse as California and South America, mudslides have destroyed homes and killed people. In 1997 two villages in the South American country of Peru were partially buried by a mudslide that occurred after several days of rain. More than three hundred people were killed in the slide, many of them buried alive as they slept.[16]

The effects of erosion are not always as dramatic as a deadly mudslide. Sometimes it takes many years before people realize what damage has been done. Erosion on hills surrounding hydroelectric projects, for example, slowly fills the lake behind the dam with soil. This reduces the amount of water in the lake and thus the amount of electricity it can produce. The soil can also be washed through the turbines of the dam, which can damage them.

Erosion also causes problems with transportation. Parts of the Panama Canal are too shallow for some very large ships because of soil that has washed into the canal from the hills surrounding it. Because of the erosion problem, large ships traveling from the East Coast to the West Coast must sail an extra ten thousand nautical miles around the southern end of South America.

The cultivation of fields for farmland can also cause erosion. Every year throughout the Western Hemisphere tons of topsoil are washed off fields and into rivers by rain. This is caused by poor farming practices that leave the soil vulnerable to erosion. In the United States, only about one-quarter of the farmland is managed to conserve soil, despite more than four decades of soil conservation efforts.[17]

Grazing can be bad for the land if too many cattle

are put in one place. The hooves of hundreds of cattle can destroy the grass, which leaves the ground vulnerable to erosion. Mismanagement of public grazing lands in the United States has left about half of that land in poor condition.[18]

Where to Dump the Trash

Ever since humans have lived in the Western Hemisphere, they have created garbage. Even the original inhabitants of the land, who wasted nothing, had to throw away some things they could not use, such as bones and shells.

The early inhabitants simply threw their waste into piles. Because there weren't many people around at the time, this wasn't a problem. But as the population grew, so did the problem of waste. Instead of creating piles of trash, people began to burn it in open dumps or incinerators or haul it out to sea where it was dumped overboard. But burning trash created air pollution, and ocean dumping created fears of water pollution. In addition, waste dumped into the ocean sometimes washed ashore.

Another option, one still being used in the 1990s, is to bury the trash in landfills. Early landfills were simply holes in the ground where trash was dumped, then covered with dirt. People hoped the trash would decompose and disappear. Instead, rain water trickling through the soil caused poisons in the trash to leak into nearby bodies of water or underground water sup-

At right, trash, a byproduct of modern life, fills acres of land at a New York City landfill. Waste disposal is a problem throughout the Western Hemisphere.

plies. Scientists studying landfills also discovered that most trash that was buried did not decompose. One researcher who dug into the Fresh Kills Landfill on Staten Island, N.Y., discovered newspapers that had been buried forty years before. The newspapers were dirty but still readable.[19]

Because the trash is not disappearing, many areas of the Western Hemisphere, especially the United States, are facing a crisis. New landfills are being built that prevent rain from leaking through the trash. These landfills are expensive, however, and they still do not solve the problem caused by mountains of trash that do not disappear. These piles can grow very large. The Fresh Kills Landfill, for example, covers more than three thousand acres of land. If all the garbage in this landfill were piled on a football field, the mound would rise almost eight miles into the sky.[20]

CHAPTER FIVE

SOLUTIONS FOR THE FUTURE

No matter how technologically advanced we become, or how much we modify our surroundings to suit our needs, we cannot escape the consequences of our actions. We must learn to care for our earth home before it becomes so dirty and worn out we can no longer live in it.

The situation, however, is not hopeless. People have begun to notice the warning signs issued by the earth and to change the way they relate to their environment. The United States has been a leader in this area, establishing the Environmental Protection Agency, which has helped to create and pass many laws designed to limit the pollution of our air and water.

Among those laws is the Clean Air Act of 1970. This law regulated the amount of pollution that could be produced by automobiles and industries. The Clean Water Act of 1972 improved water quality by requiring the use of wastewater treatment plants. These remove

At left, polluted water is purified as it passes through filters at a wastewater treatment plant.

dangerous bacteria and chemicals from city and industrial sewage before it is returned to rivers and lakes.

The United States is not alone in its efforts to protect the environment. The Canadian government has passed laws limiting air pollution that originates in Canada. Several countries in Latin America are also attempting to reduce the amount of pollution dumped into their rivers.

In addition, people are searching for better ways to dispose of waste. New incinerators are being built that reduce household trash to ash. Some of these incinerators, which have elaborate pollution controls, produce electricity as a byproduct. Because the cost of trash disposal has risen so high, many local governments in the Western Hemisphere are encouraging citizens to create less and to recycle more of their waste. This is especially true in the United States, where each person creates four pounds of trash a day.[1]

Scientists and industries are also searching for cleaner and more efficient ways to create power and use energy. Some are studying solar panels that convert sunlight into electricity. Others are investigating the use of energy created by tides or wind.

The people of the Western Hemisphere have also begun to take steps to preserve valuable natural resources, such as rain forests. In 1988, the Central American nations of Costa Rica, El Salvador, Honduras, Nicaragua, and Panama signed an agreement to set up "peace parks," in which the rain forests in their nations would be preserved. In the parks, the nations

Above, a glass recycling collection center. Many communities in the Western Hemisphere are collecting glass, paper, and other items for recycling as a way to reduce their trash.

agreed to promote only development that the fragile forests could support.[2]

Richer countries such as the United States are offering to help Central and South American nations protect the forests instead of cutting them. Costa Rica and other Western Hemisphere countries are trying to preserve their forests and make money from tourism instead of logging and destructive farming.

The United States and Canada have enacted laws recently that limit the amount of fish taken from the oceans along their shores. It is hoped that the limits will help declining fish populations grow again.

No Easy Solutions

These changes, however, do not guarantee we will live in harmony with nature anytime soon. Many of the environmental laws passed in the 1970s have been changed to allow for the creation of more pollution. Many lakes, rivers, and ocean shorelines are still too polluted to use for swimming or fishing. The air over our cities continues to contain dangerous chemicals.

In 1992, more than one hundred leaders from all over the world met at the Earth Summit in Rio de Janeiro, Brazil, to discuss air pollution, global warming, deforestation, overpopulation, and other environmental problems. At the summit's end, leaders agreed to reduce the production of greenhouse gases that contribute to global warming. The summit members also agreed to take steps to protect the habitat—in particu-

Above, wind mills in California turn wind power into energy.

Ecotourism

Several Central and South American areas are looking for new ways to make money from their famous rain forests and other natural wonders without destroying them. One way is by encouraging tourists to visit.

Ecotourism focuses on the environment of an area. Ecotourists are led through a wildlife area by specially trained guides. Unlike some guided tours, however, these trips are not luxury vacations. There is no television or electricity. Ecotourists are taken down rivers in rafts or canoes. They hike through swamps, slapping at mosquitoes along the way. At night, they bed down in tents or in crude huts.

While enduring the sometimes rough conditions, ecotourists see sights many people will never see. Visitors to the Manu region of Peru can see a section of the earth that appears to be the same today as it was hundreds of years ago when European explorers first landed in America. They can watch seventy-pound giant river otters at play and hundreds of brightly-colored macaws as they call through the forest.

Ecotourists in other regions go snorkeling over pristine coral reefs or walk through an archaeological site under study. The country makes money from tourists by charging them permit fees to visit a protected area and by selling them lodging, food, and transportation.

lar the rain forests—of species threatened by extinction.

In addition, members of the Earth Summit approved a plan, called Agenda 21, that promoted living in harmony with the earth into the twenty-first century. The plan called for development that could be supported by the earth's resources, for the use of renewable energy, and for farming methods that prevented soil erosion. At the end of the summit, the leaders proclaimed they had made great progress toward improving humanity's relationship with the earth.[3]

Five years later, in 1997, world leaders met again in New York for Earth Summit +5 to see how well the promises of the first summit were being kept. The news was not good. Despite the bold words spoken in 1992, little action had been taken in the following five years. Destruction of the world's tropical rain forests, including those in Central and South America, continued. Few countries were making serious efforts to reduce greenhouse gases.

Representatives from many countries who attended the summit said they believed the agreements reached at the 1992 Earth Summit were unfair to their countries because they were required to make greater sacrifices than others. Developing countries complained that actions to save the environment, such as reducing the use of fossil fuels, could be disastrous for nations such as Venezuela and Mexico, whose economies depend on the export of oil and other fuels.[4] Likewise, the poorer countries said they shouldn't have to bear the full cost required to establish better farming methods that will not threaten rain forests and other fragile areas.

Richer nations, such as the United States, pledged during the 1992 Earth Summit to help developing countries pay for technology that would improve the environment. But aid to developing countries has dropped from $55 billion in 1992 to less than $50 billion in 1997.[5] The drop in U.S. aid was blamed on efforts to reduce the deficit.

Many of the delegates left the 1997 summit disillusioned and angry. One environmentalist said the difficulties at the second summit were a "betrayal" of the agreements reached in 1992.[6]

No one knows what the future holds for the earth's environment. People are beginning to realize, as the original inhabitants of the Western Hemisphere knew, that we are part of the environment and that what we do has an effect that is larger than ourselves. The difficulties at the Earth Summit, however, show that there are no easy solutions to protecting the earth from the adverse effects of its inhabitants' actions.

GLOSSARY

acid rain	rain mixed with acid produced by oxides of sulfur and nitrogen in the air; created by the burning of fossil fuels
arid climate	a climate marked by little rainfall
cacao	an evergreen plant found in Central and South America; cocoa, cocoa butter, and chocolate are made from it
campesino	a small-scale farmer in Central and South America
cordillera	a chain of mountains
fluorite	a mineral used in melting down and purifying metals
fossil fuels	petroleum, coal, and other fuels created by the compression of plant and animal remains over millions of years
global warming	a theoretical phenomenon describing an overall increase in the temperature of the earth
hydroelectric power	electric power created by the force of water flowing through a turbine
isthmus	a narrow strip of land that links two larger areas of land
levee	a man-made wall to control flooding along a river
maize	corn native to the Western Hemisphere
manganese	a metallic mineral often mixed with steel and other metals to create strong, lightweight materials
methane	a gas formed by the decomposition of vegetation
molybdenum	a hard, gray metallic element used to strengthen certain kinds of metals
nitrous oxides	a combination of nitrogen and oxygen gases formed by the burning of fossil fuels
nuclear fission	the splitting of an atom that releases energy. This reaction is what happens inside a nuclear power plant.

Pan American Highway	A highway stretching sixteen thousand miles from the U.S.-Canadian border south through Central and South America to Santiago, Chile
permafrost	permanently frozen subsoil found in Arctic and subarctic climates
plateau	a level area of land that occurs at an elevation
prairie	a large grassland
rain forest	a forest with heavy and frequent rainfall and heavy growth of vegetation
seawall	a wall built next to a body of water designed to protect the land behind the wall from water damage and erosion
smog	air pollution created by sunlight acting on chemicals produced by the burning of fossil fuels in automobiles
sod	grass-covered soil
strip-mining	a method of mining in which soil is stripped from the surface of an area and minerals are removed from underneath
temperate climate	climate characterized by temperatures that vary widely between night and day and between different seasons
tropical climate	a climate characterized by warm temperatures year round and the lack of a cold winter season
tundra	an environment found at higher latitudes with a short growing season and vegetation consisting of grasses, mosses, lichens, and some small bushes
wetland	an area between dry land and open water characterized by shallow water and heavy vegetation that grows in the soil underneath

SOURCE NOTES

Chapter One: The Physical Environment

1. Farley Mowat, *People of the Deer* (New York: Pyramid Books, 1952), 18.
2. *Encyclopaedia Britannica Macropaedia,*15th ed., vol. 27 (Chicago: 1985), 482.
3. Michael D. Lemonick, "Too Few Fish in the Sea," *Time Magazine* (April 4, 1994): 70.
4. Jere Van Dyk, "The Amazon," *National Geographic Magazine,* Vol. 187, No. 2 (Washington: Feb. 1995): 38.
5. *Encyclopaedia Britannica Macropaedia,* 667.
6. "South America," *The 1995 Grolier Multimedia Encyclopedia* (Grolier Electronic Publishing, Inc., 1995).
7. Richard Brewer, *Principles of Ecology,* (Philadelphia: W.B. Saunders Company, 1979), 218.

Chapter Two: Adapting to the Environment

1. *Encyclopaedia Britannica Macropaedia,* 482.
2. Andrew H. Malcolm, *The Land and People of Canada* (New York: HarperCollins, 1991), 154.
3. *1995 Information Please Almanac* (Boston: Houghton Mifflin Co., 1995), 130.
4. Andrew H. Malcolm, *The Canadians* (New York: Times Books, 1985), 22.
5. Ibid.
6. Edgar Allen Beem, "How Cold Was It?," *Boston Globe Magazine* (Feb. 16, 1997): 24.
7. William A. Bake and James J. Kilpatrick, *The American South: Four Seasons of the Land* (Birmingham, Alabama: Oxmoor House, 1980), xxxii.
8. Ibid., xxix.
9. Pierre Etienne Dostert, *Latin America: 1995*, 29th Edition. (Harpers Ferry: W. Va.: Stryker-Post Publications, 1995), 6.
10. *1995 Information Please Almanac,* 130.
11. Ann E. Weiss, *Good Neighbors? The U.S. and Latin America* (Boston: Houghton Mifflin Co., 1985), 127.

Chapter Three: Shaping the Environment

1. Malcolm, *The Land and People of Canada,* 72.
2. "Indigenous People of the Americas," *Compton's Encyclopedia,* vol. 13 (Chicago: F.E. Compton Co., 1985), 61; and *1995 Information Please Almanac,* 677.
3. "Countries of the World," *The New York Public Library Desk Reference* (New York: Stonesong Press Inc., 1993), 853–870.
4. Kenton Miller and Laura Tangley, *Trees of Life: Saving Tropical Forests and Their Biological Wealth* (Boston, Beacon Press, 1991), 34.
5. "Forests," *The 1995 Grolier Multimedia Encyclopaedia.*
6. Thomas Y. Canby, *Our Changing Earth* (Washington: National Geographic Society, 1994), 89.
7. Miller and Tangley, *Trees of Life: Saving Tropical Forests and Their Biological Wealth,* 34.
8. Lester R. Brown, *State of the World, A Worldwatch Institute Report on Progress Toward a Sustainable Society* (New York: W.W. Norton & Company, 1992), 78.
9. I. L. Maduro Jr., *The Panama Canal* (Panama City).
10. "Environmental Impacts of Petroleum Consumption," *The 1995 Grolier Multimedia Encyclopedia.*

Chapter Four: Paying the Bill

1. Citizens for a Sound Economy web site www.cse.org/cse/eb1cw.html.
2. Peter McFarren, "Suffering City," Associated Press (March 19, 1997).
3. *Science News,* vol. 45, number 15 (April 9, 1994): 232.
4. John A. Wiens, "Oil, Seabirds and Science: The Effects of the Exxon Valdez Oil Spill," *BioScience,* vol. 48, number 8 (September 1996), 587.
5. David Campbell, "Midwest's flood-ravaged land yields bumper crops this year," Knight-Ridder News Service (November 16, 1994).
6. George Mitchell, *World on Fire: Saving an Endangered Earth* (New York: Macmillan Publishing, 1991), 14–15, 210.
7. Canby, *Our Changing Earth,* 80.

8. *Science Annual 1995* (Chicago: F.E. Compton Co., 1994), 347.
9. George Mitchell, *World on Fire: Saving an Endangered Earth,* 32.
10. Anthony Wood, "Beachfront locales in expensive battle against erosion," Knight-Ridder News Service (May 27, 1997).
12. Eugene Linden, "Endangered Earth: Biodiversity—The Death of Birth," *Time Magazine on CD-ROM* (New York: Time Inc. Magazine Co., 1995).
13. Ibid.
14. Lester R. Brown, *State of the World, A Worldwatch Institute Report on Progress Toward a Sustainable Society,* 13.
15. Ibid., 12–13.
16. "Hundreds Feared Killed by Peruvian Landslide," *New York Times* online edition (February 21, 1997).
17. Miller and Tangley, *Trees of Life: Saving Tropical Forests and Their Biological Wealth,* 16.
18. J. Madeline Nash, "The Beef Against . . . Beef," *Time Magazine on CD-ROM.*
19. William L. Rathje, "Once and Future Landfills," National Geographic Magazine, vol. 179, issue 5 (May 1991): 123.
20. Ibid.

Chapter Five: Solutions for the Future

1. Rathje, "Once and Future Landfills," 123.
2. Mitchell, *World on Fire: Saving an Endangered Earth,* 135–136.
3. Stevenson Swanson, "Summit to try to kick-start stalled international efforts to improve environment," *Chicago Tribune* (June 22, 1997). Distributed by Knight-Ridder News Service.
4. Charles J. Janley, "Summit ending on pessimistic note, with last-minute snags," Associated Press (June 27, 1997).
5. Swanson, "Summit to try to kick-start stalled international efforts to improve environment."
6. Janley, "Summit ending on pessimistic note, with last-minute snags."

FURTHER READING

Chandler, Gary, and Kevin Graham. *Making a Better World* series. New York: Twenty-First Century Books, 1996.

Duffy, Trent. *The Vanishing Wetlands.* New York: Franklin Watts, 1994.

Gay, Kathlyn. *Air Pollution.* New York: Franklin Watts, 1991.

——. *Global Garbage: Exporting Trash and Toxic Waste.* New York: Franklin Watts, 1992.

Halpern, Robert R. *Green Planet Rescue: Saving the Earth's Endangered Plants.* New York: Franklin Watts, 1993.

Herda, D. J. *Environmental America: The Northeastern States.* Brookfield: The Millbrook Press, 1991.

Hoff, Mary, and Mary M. Rodgers. *Our Endangered Planet: Rivers and Lakes.* Minneapolis: Lerner Publications Co., 1991.

Law, Kevin J. *Know Your Government: The Environmental Protection Agency.* New York: Chelsea House, 1988.

Macdonald, Fiona. *Houses: Habitats & Home Life.* New York: Franklin Watts, 1994.

McClung, Robert M. Last *Wild America, The Story of Our Extinct and Vanishing Wildlife.* Hamden, Conn.: Linnet Books, 1993.

Miller, Kenton, and Laura Tangley. *Trees of Life: Saving Tropical Forests and their Biological Wealth.* Boston: Beacon Press, 1991.

Mitchell, George J. *World on Fire: Saving an Endangered Earth.* New York: Charles Scribner's Sons, 1991.

Pringle, Laurence. *Global Warming; Assessing the Greenhouse Threat.* New York: Little Brown and Company, 1990.

Sayre, April Pulley. *Exploring Earth's Biomes* series. New York: Twenty-First Century Books, 1996.

Winckler, Suzanne, and Mary M. Rodgers. *Our Endangered Planet: Population Growth.* Minneapolis: Lerner Publications Co., 1991.

INDEX

acid rain, 6, 70–71, 89
agriculture, 6, 16, 21–22, 26, 28, 33, 36–37, 41, 43, 46, 50–52, 66, 68, 73–74, 78–79, 85, 87–89
air pollution, 6, *68*, 68–71, 79, 84–85, 90
Alaskan Highway, 54
Amazon River, 11, *29*, 29–30, 32–33, 47, 54
Andes Mountains, 5, *29*, 29–31, *30*, *34*, 35, 47
Appalachian mountain system (U.S.), 17–18, *18*, 21
Appalachian Region (Canada), *12*, 13–14
Arctic plains, *12*, 13
Atlantic Plain, 17–18, *18*
Baja California peninsula, *23*, 24
Balsas Depression, *23*, 25
Barrens, 12
Brazilian Highlands, 31
Canada, *4*, 5, 9–19, *12*, *18*, 21–22, 35–41, 43, 51–54, 60–61, 69–71, 73–75, 84–85, 90
    climate, 11, 13–15, 36, 39
    lands, 11–13
    lifestyle, 37, 39–40
    natural resources, 15–17
    people, 35–36
    rainfall, 14–15
    vegetation, 15–17, *16*
Canadian Cordillera, *12*, 13
Canadian Shield, 11–13, *12*, 15
Cascade mountain range, *18*, 19, *60*
cattle ranching (*see* grazing)
Central America, *4*, 9–11, *23*, 27–29, *29*, 38, 44–45, 49, 52–55, 64, 70, 73–74, 84–87, 89–90
    climate, 11, 27–28, 44
    lands, 27
    lifestyle, 45–46
    natural resources, 28
    people, 44–45
    rainfall, 27–28
    vegetation, *27*, 28
Choqueyapu River, 64
Clean Air Act of 1970, 83
Clean Water Act of 1972, 83
Colorado Plateau, *18*, 19
Cuyahoga River, 64
dams, 6, 10, 50, 56, 59-61, *60*, 78
Earth Summit (1992), 85, 87–88
Earth Summit +5, 87–88
ecotourism, 85, 86
El Popo (*see* Popocatepetl)
energy (*see also* fossil fuels, hydropower, nuclear power, petroleum), 6, 50, 57–61, 72, 84–85, 87, 89
    alternative, 84, *85*
Environmental Protection Agency (U.S.), 83
erosion, 76–79, *77*, 87, 90
Europeans
    attitude toward environment, 6, 49–50, 73
    in the Western Hemisphere, 5–6, 43, 49–51, 57, 75, 86
Exxon Valdez, 58, 65
farming (*see* agriculture)
flooding
    control measures, 55–57
    damage, 6–7, 56, 63, 65–67, 72, 89
forests (*see also* rain forests), 6–7, *15*, 15–16, 21–22, 25–26, 28, 32, 46, 59, 67, 71, 76, 85–86, 90
    loss of, 50–52, *51*, *52*, 73–74, 85
fossil fuels 57, 63, 68–71, 89–90
Fresh Kills Landfill, 80–81
global warming (*see also* greenhouse gases), 71–73, 85
Grand Canyon, *19*, 19
Grand Forks, North Dakota, 67
grazing, 22, 26, 32–33, 50–53, 73, 78–79
Great Lakes-St. Lawrence Lowlands, *12*, 13–14
Great Plains, 12, *18*, 18, 20–21, 38
greenhouse gases (*see also* global warming), *72*, 85, 87
Gulf Coastal Plain, 24–25, *25*
Hoover Dam, 59
housing, 38, 50, 52, 56, 63, 67
    in Canada, 36–40
    in Central America, 38, *45*, 45–46

in Mexico, 43–44
in South America, 47
in United States, 38, 42
hydropower, 50, 59–60, *60*
Incas, *30*, 49
Inuit, 38–40
Itaipu Dam, 60
landfills (*see also* waste disposal), 71, 79–81, *80*
Latin America, 9, 23, 44–45, 84
Maritimes (*see also* Appalachian Region), 13, 36
Mayans, 38, 45, 49
Mexican Plateau, *23*, 23, 25–26
Mexico, *4*, 9–10, 17, *18*, 22–27, *23*, *25*, 40, *43*, 43–44, 49, 53, 68–69, 87
climate, 23, *25*, 25–26, 43–44
lands, 22–25
lifestyle, 43–44
natural resources, 25–27
people, 43
rainfall, 25
vegetation, 25–27
Mexico City, *40*, 43, *68*, 69
mining, 16, 18, 33, 35, *58*, 58, 61, 90
Mississippi River, 11, *18*, 54
mudslides (*see also* erosion), 77–78
Native Americans (Indians), 6, 38–39, 44–46, 49–50, 56–57, 79, 88
attitude toward environment, 5–6, 49
New York City, *40*, 55, *80*, 80, 87
North America, *4*, 9–11, 17, 23, 28, *43*, *51*, 51–52, 70, 73–74 (*see also* Canada, Central America, Mexico, United States)
nuclear power, 60–61, *61*, 89
oil spills, 58, *63*, 63–65
Orinoco River, *29*, 29, 31
overfishing, 74–76
ozone, 69–70
Pacific coastal lowlands, 24
Panama Canal, 27, *55*, 55, 78
Pan American Highway, 54, 90
Patagonian plateaus, *29*, 29
peace parks, 84–85
petroleum, 17, 22, 26–27, 33, 42, 57–59, 65, 68–69, 87, 89
pollution (*see* air pollution, water pollution, waste disposal)
Popocatepetl volcano (El Popo), *23*, 24
rain forests, 5, 7, 21–22, 25, 27–33, 46–47, 52–54, 72–74, 76, 84, 86–88, 90
recycling, *84*, 84
Rio de Janeiro, 47
Rocky Mountains, *12*, 12–13, *18*, 18, 20–21
São Paulo, *40*, 47
smog (*see also* air pollution), 68–70, 90
South America, *4*, 5, 9–11, *23*, 28–33, *29*, 46–47, 49, 52–55, 64, 69–70, 73–74, 76–78, 85–87, 89–90
climate, 30–31, 47
lands, 29–30
lifestyle, 46–47
natural resources, 31–33
people, *34*, 46
rainfall, 30–31
vegetation, 31–33
Southern Highlands, 25
species loss, 7, 73–74, 75–76, 87
Toronto, *36*, 37
transportation, 36, 53–55, 57, 63, 78, 86
in Canada, 37, 39, 53
in Central America, 53–55, 90
in Mexico, 43–44, 53
in South America, 53–55, 90
in United States, 41, 43, 53–55, 90
United States, *4*, 5, 9-10, *12*, 12-13, 17, *18*, 19-22, *23*, 26, 35-41, 43, 51-54, 59-61, 69-74, 78-80, 83-85, 88
climate, 19–21, 40–43, 60
lands, 17–19
lifestyle, 41–43
natural resources, 21–22
people, 40–41
rainfall, 20–21
vegetation, 21–22
volcanoes, 19, *20*, 23-24, 27-28
waste disposal, 6, *61*, 61, 64, 71, 79-81, *80*, *84*, 84
water pollution, *64*, 64–65, 70, 79, *82*, 83, 85
West Indies, 10, *23*, *27*, 28
Western Cordillera (U.S.), *18*, 18
wetlands, 6, 56, 65, 90
Yucatan Peninsula, *23*, 24–25, *25*